IDOLS
OF OUR TIME

Bob Goudzwaard
Foreword by Howard A. Snyder

Translated by
Mark Vander Vennen

INTER-VARSITY PRESS
DOWNERS GROVE
ILLINOIS 60515

Originally published in 1981 as Genoodzaakt goed te wezen by Uitgeversmaatschappij J. H. Kok. English translation © 1984 by Inter-Varsity Christian Fellowship of the United States of America.

InterVarsity Press is the book-publishing division of Inter-Varsity Christian Fellowship, a student movement active on campus at hundreds of universities, colleges and schools of nursing. For information about local and regional activities, write IVCF, 233 Langdon St., Madison, WI 53703.

Distributed in Canada through InterVarsity Press, 860 Denison St., Unit 3, Markham, Ontario L3R 4H1, Canada.

All Scripture quotations, unless otherwise noted, are taken from the Holy Bible: New International Version, copyright © 1978 by the New York International Bible Society. Used by permission of Zondervan Bible Publishers.

Cover illustration: Marcus Hamilton

ISBN 0-87784-970-6

Printed in the United States of America

Library of Congress Cataloging in Publication Data

Goudzwaard, B.
    Idols of our time.

    Translation of: Genoodzaakt goed te wezen.
    Includes bibliographical references.
    1. Hope–Religious aspects–Christianity.   2. Civili-
zation, Modern–20th century.   3. Church and the world.
I. Title.
BV4638.G6813   1984   261'.09'04   84-652
ISBN 0-87784-970-6

| 17 | 16 | 15 | 14 | 13 | 12 | 11 | 10 | 9 | 8 | 7 | 6 | 5 | 4 | 3 | 2 | 1 |
| 97 | 96 | 95 | 94 | 93 | 92 | 91 | 90 | 89 | 88 | 87 | 86 | 85 | 84 | | | |

FOREWORD

Toward the end of this intriguing book the author invokes the image of Esther, "the Morning Star," whose act of sacrificial obedience saved a people. Reminding us that Jesus Christ is the Morning Star, the star of hope (Rev 22:16), the author calls Christians today to renounce the demonic ideologies of power, prosperity, revolution and nationalism, and to take the critical steps of sacrificial obedience which, like the Morning Star, can herald the dawn of God's New Day.

Goudzwaard is right. We *do* live in an age of ideologies, and these ideologies have come to possess us. To an alarming degree, Christians are idolators. As the author carefully shows, the goals of prosperity, security, might and nation have all the classical marks of an ideology. Thus they have become our gods. And business as usual in the church is not going to save us as long as foreign gods are set up in our sanctuaries.

Goudzwaard unmasks the idols. He unravels the ideologies which we blindly accept as simply "good political sense." And, finally, he points toward some solutions.

Particularly intriguing are the author's proposals in the final chapter. What would happen if we created economies of *care* and economies of *enough,* rather than economies of exploitation, destruction and growth at all costs? There *is* another way, and it would work. Today's national economies "work" by spending huge sums on weapons of destruction. Redirecting a significant proportion of these resources toward cancelling the debts of poor nations and reclaiming our own cities and environment would work just as well—better, in fact—and would "reverse the spiral" leading to disaster, sparking instead international peace, stability and community.

It all makes sense, and it must be heard.

This book is a significant addition to the small but growing chorus of voices in the church today calling us away from our ideologies and idolatries and back to God's law and promise for justice on earth. I hope it will be heard and heeded.

Howard A. Snyder

CHAPTER 1

In the
Shadows
of Progress

"WE LIVE IN A WORLD POSSESSED. AND WE KNOW IT."

With these words the famous Dutch historian Johan Huizinga opened his book *In the Shadows of Tomorrow* in 1935.[1] By then the Nazis next door had taken Germany's democracy into their own hands. Bleak clouds had gathered over Europe and over the world. The forces which led to World War 2 had already been set in motion, and they cast long, dark shadows. And Huizinga caught those forces in that short expression: "a world possessed."

It is now nearly fifty years later. The violence of World War 2 has swept over us, and on the rubble a world has been built which at first glance hardly resembles the world of 1935. What a stunning explosion of knowledge, information, communication and production has erupted in Western society in just a few, short years! Our means of rapid transportation have mushroomed, shrinking the world into a global village. Satellites circle above us; deep-sea divers harvest manganese turnips below us. Science controls the process of splitting the nucleus, searches for black holes and pulsars, and stands on the verge of manipulating human genes. And Western material prosperity has more than doubled. Today we surround ourselves with washing machines, television sets, microwave ovens and even computers—household items which our grandparents could only dream about.

Perhaps the obvious conclusion is that Huizinga's description of his world is no longer appropriate today. Progress has made it obsolete. "A world possessed" is a world overrun by irrationality, by terror-crazed ideologies and by the demonic. And for us the spectacular explosion of human expertise and productivity in the last fifty years may suggest the triumph of rationality and control. As the opposite of irrationality, it is a sign of liberation from the shadows of the thirties.

But our situation is not so simple. Along with the advances of the last fifty years a host of unsolved problems have arisen. Today we face high unemployment *and* high inflation, the permanent and increasing loneliness of many in our society and repeated outbursts of violence on our streets. We also encounter the persistent needs of the poorest countries, whose burden of debt is soaring, dwindling respect for the fragility of human life and the environment, and an unbelievable arms race, which grows frighteningly more entrenched. Unlike before, these problems cannot be solved by adding a few extra tricks, injecting a little more expertise or raising productivity. In the last fifty years they have become rigid or "structural." Economists today debate structural unemployment *and* structural inflation, and structural balance of payment deficits in the poorest countries. Sociologists have developed theories describing structural alienation and structural violence, which occur on both urban and world scales. Biologists express concern over the structural annihilation of the world ecosystem. Polemologists (people who study war and peace) such as Alva Myrdal, a long-time peace negotiator, argue that the arms problem is structural.

In other words, in the last fifty years our expertise and production capacity have skyrocketed, but the rigidity of our problems has increased proportionately.

Some scientists and technicians still pretend that the cure for our society's ailments lies in their growing expertise. But in the face of our overwhelming structural problems their voices sound more and more haggard, stilted, less convincing and aimed at covering up past mistakes. Psychiatrist's offices overflow, and many of us no longer plan for the future. We lapse into fatalism or withdraw into our own small worlds. Today there seem to be forces at work which systematically push our problems out of our grasp and over our heads.

Is it possible that the persistence of our problems means that our world is still "a world possessed"? Do ideologies as powerful as the Nazi ideology have a place in our lives today?

Let us dig deeper into the novelty of our situation. For the first time in history most of our problems deteriorate the moment we try to solve them. Our *solutions* intensify the problems they were intended to solve or create new and more serious problems.

For example, since the thirties, government has fought unemployment by increasing the buying power in society. In general, however, unemployment no longer responds to more injections of capital. Today job creation along these lines requires a *vast* dosage of capital. Over the years the repeated treatments have stimulated enormous advances in production technology and the resulting capital intensity of production processes.

Similarly, the problem of national security is oblivious to past solutions, such as an increase in armaments. When countries all around the world accept arms escalation as *the* prescription for security, the result is that global insecurity increases, the world's most vital resources become more scarce and countries falter under larger and larger doses of weapons expenditures. And the cure for these problems does *not* lie in higher productivity or more technical expertise.

Technology no longer solves the environmental problem either. Of course, it is possible to develop technologies which counteract erosion and which clean the environment. But developing such technologies does not help if at the same time we use increasingly efficient technologies to sacrifice the world's virgin forests to our growing wood and paper needs. Nor do such technologies help when the depletion of world energy reserves drives us to pursue the most technologically advanced forms of nuclear energy, an energy source hazardous to air and water. Conservation of the environment is then like trying to drain a flood without repairing the leak.

How strange that our solutions—economic growth, technological development, the advance of the applied sciences and the expansion of the state—have also hardened our problems! Our solutions have turned against us, at least in part. Gradually they have gained independence and autonomy from us. They still alleviate poverty and disease, improve crops, develop faster means of transportation and so forth. But the problems they leave in their wake—traffic congestion in cities, chronic welfare dependency, the fall of the poorest countries into deeper hunger and dependence, loss of control over the arms race and the bureaucratization of the state—are often more serious and more structural than the problems they solve. In certain respects the forces of growth have become more powerful than us. As Karl Löwith once lamented: "Progress itself goes on progressing; we can no longer stop it or turn it around."[2]

Our Gods Have Betrayed Us

Where did this autonomy of technology, science, the economy and the state come from? Did it happen by itself? Nothing happens on its own. Did fate bring it upon us? That possibility is highly remote. Perhaps instead our world is "a world possessed."

In very brief strokes I shall suggest the answer which I defend in the following chapters. We know from Scripture that both persons and societies can put their faith in things or forces which their own hands have made. In their pursuit of prosperity, salvation, health, protection and so forth, people sooner or later create gods. But gods never leave their makers alone. Because people put themselves in a position of dependence on their gods, invariably the moment comes when those things or forces gain the upper hand. The things or forces control their creators as idols, as gods who can betray their makers. It is conceivable then that the means to progress which our own hands have made—the economy, technology, science and the state—have become such forces today, imposing their will on us as gods.

This suggestion is not as far-fetched as it sounds. Suppose we take an example. Societies can become so dependent on the means which they create for bringing material prosperity that those means take on their own life and are elevated above their makers. If we examine an issue like structural unemployment, for example, we quickly realize that the problem of unemployment today is tied to the pattern and rate of economic growth. For years in Western society we have seen economic growth as *the* way to achieve greater material prosperity. This move has made us wealthier, but also more defenseless. The unquestioned necessity of economic growth means that our production factors,

labor and capital, must be of maximum efficiency and must lead
to the highest possible growth. If the machine or robot can work
more efficiently than labor, then we eliminate employment opportunities. In 1980 Japan opened the first factory where robots
make new robots—robots are less costly and more efficient than
people. Such are the dictates of continuous economic growth.
Yet all of us submit to these dictates in the name of our highest
goal or end: greater material prosperity. Structural unemployment is the tragic but inescapable consequence. It is the price
which economic progress exacts of us.

How can economic growth so rudely tell us what to do? Is
industry to blame? I believe that this answer is too easy. It strikes
me that the blame lies with us. In the name of material prosperity
we have yielded our responsibility to the perceived source of our
prosperity. Unchallenged economic growth, an idol made by our
own hands, has become a power which forces its will on us. Christians and non-Christians alike, *possessed by an end* (material prosperity), have allowed various forces, means and powers in our
society (for example, untrammeled economic growth) to rule
over us as gods.

The Lesson of the Stone
In the following chapters we shall explore the possibility that
similar "goal possessions" lie at the foundation of most of our
society's problems, from growing unemployment to violence on
the streets, and from abortion and environment crises to the arms
race. And we shall find that continuous economic growth is one
example of an idol among many. But first we must introduce
another issue: hope. For in the face of autonomous, tyrannical
powers, our hope may vanish. What is the meaning of hope today? Is there any hope of defeating these powers?

For many people hope lies in overthrowing the public structures of society. Their litany is familiar: away with the militaristic state; away with multinational corporations; away with large-scale technologies; away with nuclear weapons and nuclear energy; away too with experts and technicians, who issue the oracles of the day. These people will sympathize with any new crusade to destroy whatever floods or brainwashes us, as, for example, the modern communications media do. But they have failed to see that the enemy is not technology, the economy, science, the state or the corporation as such. The *real* enemy lies within *ourselves;* we who on occasion transform these powers into tyrannical idols. Campaigns of this nature only pull people into the same force field that they wish to oppose. The enthusiasm of a new revolution only disappears in a new iconoclasm. Full-scale revolution is simply prostration before perpetual violence—an idol even more tyrannical and merciless than the forces of progress.

Others in our society have lost all hope. Deathly afraid of possible unemployment, nuclear war and the ruin of the environment, they have become fatalists. These calamities may indeed come. But they will strike us only if we continue to sustain the forces threatening to make them realities.

When the real enemy comes into focus, our courage may sink down to our toes. But at that moment a strategy also opens up for hitting the enemy at its weak point. Just as centuries ago David found a smooth stone to sling at Goliath, so we too must find a stone to fling at the enemy today. And like David, we have the assurance that such a stone lies within our reach.

Times which deserve the label "a world possessed" are not times without hope. Fatalism, expertise and mass revolution threaten to extinguish hope. But genuine hope is deeper than these threats. It flares up just when the night is at its darkest.

CHAPTER 2

Ideology
and
Idolatry

IN THE LAST CHAPTER I INTRODUCED THE PHRASE *POSSESSED BY an end.* I suggested that this possession lies at the foundation of the most vexing problems of our society and also allows idols to impose their will on us. To explain this suggestion, I must introduce another term: *ideology.* Though the discussion of ideology here may seem abstract, I shall be more concrete when we study ideologies in action in chapters three through six.

Ideology

The word *ideology* is not new. It was coined during the Enlightenment, shortly before the French Revolution of 1789. The theorists of the revolution used *ideology* to describe their revolutionist world of ideas. The word therefore means much more than simply a framework of thought—the common definition of *ideology* today. In its original sense, ideology means an entire system of values, conceptions, convictions and norms which are used as a set of tools for reaching a single, concrete, all-encompassing societal end.

The Ideology of Revolution. The all-controlling aim of the French Enlightenment thinkers was to overthrow the existing empire of church and nobility (the *ancien régime,* an oppressive, feudal regime). Their ideology was therefore an ideology of revolution. For them the goal of overturning the old regime was so sweeping and decisive that it legitimized in advance every means for reaching that end. They had no desire to ask whether a violent overthrow of the regime or the mass murder of the nobility under the guillotine was in keeping with the basic requirements of justice, freedom and the love of one's neighbor. What the revolution required was *by definition* legitimate; unquestionably it served the cause of freedom and genuine brotherhood. Existing norms and values were therefore emptied, refilled, tainted and warped until they became instruments of the all-embracing goal. "No God, no master" was the slogan of this ideology. Enlightened reason, which would decide what was good and evil for humanity, replaced God and spurred the French on to total revolution.

This redefinition of norms is what characterizes an ideology. Ideology turns all existing norms into coworkers instead of opponents. It defines goodness, truth, justice and love as that which serves the end. In its original sense, therefore, ideology has everything to do with religion. It is religion's substitute. Ideology says: "As God I create my own norms and values. I say what will benefit humanity. And I allow no god above or power below to make any other law." Ideology is an attempt at the re-creation of life with the material of a new source of meaning. Its origin therefore lies in the *demonic.*

Other Ideologies. Naturally, the ideology of revolution is not the only possible ideology. I may set my heart on the revolutionary overthrow of an old society and the creation of a new one. But I may also attempt to preserve an *existing* society with all the means at my disposal. Then too I will bend the norms of truth, justice and love until they become unwitting collaborators in the manipulation and perversion of the hearts of people. "The Party is always right," said the Nazis. The Party was able to fashion its own "right" because of Nazi commitment to one, concrete goal: the protection of Hitler's regime within the framework of a vast Germanic empire. Similarly, when Mussolini came to power he used biblical terms like *faith* and *obedience* to articulate the new morality of Italy. In a speech in Florence in 1923 Mussolini stated: "When a *faith* is consecrated in the red blood of the youth, we cannot fail, we cannot die, we will not die."[1]

So far these examples sound familiar to us but do not touch us personally. Few among us feel kinship with the aims of the French Revolution or the dreams of Nazi and fascist barbarianism. Their goals and dreams are not ours. But what about the pursuit of *our* goals and the fulfillment of *our* deepest dreams? How far are we ourselves prepared to go in reaching our highest ends and ideals? Where does pursuing a legitimate goal end and an ideology begin?

Four Dominant Goals. Suppose we identify the major goals or ends which occupy people around the world today and then determine whether they have become ideologies. We may find that these goals occupy us too. They may give life meaning and purpose to those who pursue them. There are at least four:

1. The resistance of all exploiting and oppressive powers in order to create a better society.

2. The survival of one's people or nation: the preservation of one's hard-fought freedoms and/or cultural identity.

3. The preservation of one's wealth or prosperity, and the opportunity for continued material progress.

4. Guaranteed security: the protection of oneself, one's children and one's fellow human beings against any attack from outside.

No one would maintain that these goals are illegitimate in and of themselves, or that they may not be pursued in any way. One goal probably appeals more to one person, and the other to another. But an ideology does not arise because of the *illegitimacy* of a goal. One may even say that the more legitimate a goal seems, the more likely an ideology will eventually anchor itself in the hearts of men and women. Legitimate goals *can* turn into ideologies.

In the following chapters we shall see that today's dominant ends have in fact become genuine ideologies. Ideologies of revolution, nation, material prosperity and guaranteed security surround us. To various degrees, Christians have aided them in the past and still contribute to them today, each doing so in his or her own way.

Idolatry
When then does pursuing a legitimate goal become ideological? We may offer a partial answer here: an ideology arises when *idolatry* takes root in the pursuit of a legitimate end. The presence of idolatry indicates the presence of an ideology. We would do well then to look at idolatry in more detail.

Idol worship is something which no Christian wants. Along with those of the Jewish faith, Christians realize that serving idols violates God's covenant. God has made a covenant with his people that if they hold no other gods before his face, he will lead them out of the house of bondage and slavery. Idol worship—breaking the human end of the covenant—is therefore directly related to the symptoms of diseased life within the house of slavery, namely, distress, oppression and fear. Those symptoms are all around us, here and now. Does idol worship surround us then too?

Suppose we consider the worship of a wood, stone or porcelain image, a practice still common in the world today. This worship has several steps. First, people sever something from their immediate environment, refashion it and erect it on its own feet in a special place. Second, they ritually consecrate it and kneel before it, seeing it as a thing which has life in itself. Third, they bring sacrifices and look to the idol for advice and direction. In short, they worship it. Worship brings with it a decrease in their own power; now the god reveals how they should live and act. And fourth, they expect the god to repay their reverence, obedience and sacrifices with health, security, prosperity and happiness. They give the idol permission to demand and receive whatever it desires, even if it includes animal or human life, because they see the idol as their savior, as the one who can make life whole and bring blessing.

Technology as an Idol.   Nothing in these steps suggests that an idol is always a physical thing or a comical piece of wood or stone. Idolatry is not that superficial. I can illustrate this with a contemporary example of an idol.

Technology, or the art of making tools, is surely a fruit of God's good creation. It is not evil—modern doomsday thinkers to the contrary. But both nations and persons can grant technology its own life and set it on its own course. Convincing themselves that what technology *can* do it *must* do, some may demand that we adapt indiscriminately to the requirements of modern technology. To them unrestricted technology offers a better life, more luxury, more prosperity and better health, not to mention solutions to a number of current world problems. Others may entrust to unhampered technological development their deepest security needs, believing that superior weapons technology insulates them from the hands of any possible enemy. To these persons and nations technology has then become an idol. And because they adapt that idol to our dynamic culture, technology needs constant development. They make room for this development in our society, even if they must sacrifice, because they believe that technology gives life meaning.

The parallel between technology as an idol and primitive idol worship runs even deeper. We all know that fear plays an important role in idolatry. Fear arises because gradually the roles of idol and idol worshiper undergo a reversal. First, people make an idol. They fashion an image however they wish. Soon, however, they become dependent on their own creation. No wonder: having given the creation its own life, it has a grip on them. The slightest misstep can trigger the wrath of the idol, a wrath which may even bring them to ruin. This dependence of the maker on his idol is the result of a complete role reversal. Now the idol imprints its image on the maker, not vice versa. Though people make an image, eventually they bear the image of what they have made. The psalms graphically describe this change:

[Idols] have mouths, but cannot speak,
    eyes, but they cannot see;
they have ears, but cannot hear,
    noses, but they cannot smell;
they have hands, but cannot feel,
    feet, but they cannot walk;
    nor can they utter a sound with their throats.
Those who make them will be like them,
    and so will all who trust in them.[2]

We may add this role reversal to the four steps we listed previously and call it the fifth step of idol worship. When the reversal is complete, fear becomes the chief characteristic of life.

Now, certainly it may be said that an irrational fear of technology exists today. Further, a reversal of roles seems to have taken place. Are we not just digits in a computer? That is what we read in magazines and newspapers. As if computers were alive! In industry humans are adjusted to the machine and its tempo; the machine is not usually adjusted to human creativity and the rhythms of human life. Modern men and women feel more that technology controls them than that they control technology. Are these coincidences, or signs that technology occupies an exaggerated, perhaps idolatrous place in modern society?

Ideology: The Conduit of Idolatry

Now we may return to answer the question of when the pursuit of a legitimate goal becomes an ideology. An ideology arises in the midst of that pursuit the moment that the *end* indiscriminately justifies every *means*. This blanket justification gives the means *power,* and they then turn into idols. An obsession with a goal—ideology—legitimates the means. The means then gradually become idols. The goal of material prosperity, for example, justifies the means of continuous economic and technological expansion. It justifies these means with a vast system of redefined norms and values. Ideology is therefore related to idolatry as the end is related to the means. We might say then that ideology is the conduit, track or channel along which idolatry comes to life and moves.

An ideology never rests until its end is reached. Therein lies its strength (it leaves nothing untouched to reach the end) and its weakness (it embraces every means necessary for achieving that end). It may, for example, enlist technology to guarantee security or recruit the social sciences to rationalize an expanding state. Technology and science then have power. They are the levers of change. But their power is not in the hands of its users. Instead, science and technology have power over them. They must be obeyed, because they lead to the goal. If they perpetuate injustice, hatred, the abuse of the environment, or even if they require human sacrifice, then we will distort the biblical mandates of justice, love and stewardship. If need be we will call injustice "justice," dictatorship "freedom," and annihilation "the saving of life." Ideology is therefore falsehood; it twists truth, freedom and justice for the sake of a disproportionate goal.

The means then lord it over their users, becoming powers under their own control. As if these means were skilled ventriloquists, many of today's technicians, scientists and experts mouth their new standard of life: total devotion to technological, economic, scientific and political means to prosperity and survival. As gifts of the creation transformed into autonomous powers, these means are the hidden idols of today.

The Complete Ideology

In the chapters to come we shall subject today's ideologies to a test. It is a test of completeness. We shall look for the trademarks of the full-fledged ideology. The mature ideology carries at least five trademarks:

1. The end has extraordinary significance. The goal affects people so deeply that they will fight for it to excess, if necessary.

2. The means work without restriction. Biblical norms do not hold the means in check. Instead, the ideology judges the means by the test of maximum effectiveness for reaching the end.

3. The end distorts genuine norms and values. They are filled with a new content until they become useful instruments in motivating people to pursue the end. This distortion especially affects Christ's commands to walk in his truth, to do justice, and to love our neighbor as ourselves. The distortion of *these* norms

betrays an ideology. For with them an ideology touches the human heart and reveals itself as false revelation.

4. The end demands that men, women and the environment continually adjust to the new laws of the continually developing means. If some aspect of the environment or humankind is ruined, this is justified as an unfortunate but necessary sacrifice for the good cause: the happiness of all.

5. The end creates its own false enemies. The ideology declares anyone a traitor who because of his position or past forms an obstacle to the goal. The ideology displays an artificial image of the enemy. The image will not be accurate; its suitability lies only in its usefulness to the goal. The ideology therefore creates scapegoats, who like the Jews under German occupation bear the blame for all the evils which still exist in society.

If an ideology bears these trademarks, it is full-fledged. And if its means have become full-grown gods—if all the steps of idolatry are completed—the range of the ideology is total or absolute. As uncontrollable powers these gods incite fear, a feeling of massive dependence or even slavery, and a steady stream of sacrifices.

Why am I so harsh on ideology? Because I meet an imitation Christianity in a genuine, full-fledged ideology. The mature ideology is a false revelation of creation, fall and redemption. In a certain sense it recreates humanity and the world. Identifying its own source of sin, it erects its own antithesis between good and evil. And it promises the redemption of life. It speaks too of necessary suffering and sacrifice—sometimes bloody sacrifice—which the predetermined goal legitimates. In a certain way, therefore, an ideology imitates the suffering and death of the Messiah.

Ideology and Us
Ideology, idolatry—these words sound not only terribly heavy

but also miles removed from us and from our own world. Perhaps we feel angry at the accusation that we may have something to do with them. Certainly we ordinary people, we Westerners, are not possessed, goal crazed or fanatic! Even the suggestion goes too far.

But the distance between us and ideology is not as huge as we may think. To begin with, an ideology does not need a broad base of support to exist. It can prosper on a small scale in your life or mine. All of us know of times when a certain goal takes on extraordinary importance for us. We may feel threatened by the possible loss of a job, a child, a spouse or money, or we may set our heart on acquiring something which suddenly seems within reach. Then we utilize everything at our disposal to reach our goal. The goal becomes something that we pursue with all the strength we can muster. If necessary we adjust our standards a little—just as the dominant ideologies do—in order to give us more room to act as we like. The persons or things whose help we need to reach our goal suddenly become uncommonly important. Gradually we become dependent on them, and because of our dependence they gain power over us. If they wish, they can manipulate us and even make humiliating demands. If for the sake of our goal we comply, then those persons or things have become our gods. The roles have been reversed: self-governing powers control us for as long as our dependence exists and our goal is not reached.

Furthermore, all the dominant ideologies have their origin in immediate and personal circumstances. They almost always arise in situations where something basic is lacking. For example, an ideology may arise in a situation of horrible injustice, as it did in France shortly before the French Revolution, when the pact of the church and nobility ravaged the rural communities. Or an ideology may arise in a situation of great external threat, as when a foreign enemy threatens our nation's existence and everything we cherish within it. Or again an ideology may arise in a situation of terrible poverty, which, if not eliminated, would cause the deaths of ourselves and our families. Without such deep-seated causes an ideology will not generate a genuine movement. It anchors itself in something which is fundamentally wrong or which threatens people mercilessly. Because it offers an alternative, often a utopian alternative, an ideology grips the hearts and behavior of people. From that point on, people will consider legitimate any means of breaking out of their awful impasse.

We must remember the modest origins of ideology as we consider the dominant ideologies of our time. For today's ideologies are not small, static systems but forces whose powerful momentum pushes us along also.

CHAPTER 3

The
Ideology of
Revolution

WHEN THE IDEOLOGY OF REVOLUTION REARS ITS HEAD, IT always strikes at what is basically unjust. This has been true both in the past and today.

For example, the Russian Revolution of 1917 erupted in a period when the feudal lords of the Russian farmlands not only treated the peasants like slaves but also sold them like slaves. The gentry were taxed by the number of peasants they owned, a practice which Gogol satirized in his sardonic novel *Dead Souls*.[1] Protected by the religious umbrella of the Russian Orthodox Church, the czar ruled as an absolute dictator, as a divinely chosen ruler to whose caprices everyone was subject. Men and women died like rats, both inside and outside of prison. In this bleak and seemingly hopeless situation the revolution ideology easily took hold, gradually claiming large segments of the population. Russia had

had a long history of revolutionary movements even before Marxism/Leninism came on the scene.

Anyone with a knowledge of current world affairs recognizes the same situation today. In Latin America many people suffer terribly in tiny shanties or vanish silently, invisible victims of the security police and the terrorist groups which work under police auspices. Inside the prisons people are tortured; outside they are terrorized by three cooperating powers: the state (often a military dictatorship), some or most of the church dignitaries, who shield their eyes from the injustice, and the economic power-brokers, especially the wealthy families with vast land holdings. In such countries multinational corporations often feel like fish in water, because where order and authority reign, business is good.

If in the midst of such circumstances liberation movements arise, the fault lies with the oppressive regimes themselves. When people's basic living circumstances and primary rights are interfered with to so great an extent, resistance is almost unavoidable. In such situations people may even have a right to resist. The Reformer John Calvin recognized a right of rebellion under strict conditions, and the United States owes its existence to its forebears' exercise of that right. Groen van Prinsterer, leader of the Dutch antirevolutionary movement in the nineteenth century, wrote: "I too covet the word 'revolutionary,' if revolution means a just reformation carried out according to the demands of time and circumstance."[2] But a caution is still necessary. At a given moment the pursuit of a justifiable end, such as banishing a dictator or erecting a more just social order, can become an overarching, legitimating goal and expand into an ideology, an ideology which has no flexibility in its use of means and which mobilizes forces that gradually slip out of control.

The communist revolution ideology is a good illustration of

the ideology of revolution. Though begun on a limited scale, in the course of time it grew into a full-fledged, absolute and dominant ideology. It granted its means their own life, means which today tyrannize and trample on people and the environment.

Marxism/Leninism

Many distinguished and convinced communists have become bitter over and alienated from contemporary communism, especially communism behind the Iron Curtain. They feel that communism in practice has come into conflict with its own ideals. The Pole Leszek Kolakowski, the Yugoslav Milovan Djilas and the East German Rudolf Bahro—to name a few—all come to the conclusion that the oppression in their countries was never the intention of Marx and his original colleagues.[3] Their thesis presents us with a puzzling dilemma. For if oppression was not the intention of Marx, then where did the oppression within *all* Marxist countries come from?

Marx himself never wanted to use the word *ideology* to describe the scientific socialism or communism he advocated. Instead, he used the word to show that within bourgeois society the elite promotes and upholds a false consciousness—an ideology—in order to justify its own position. The ideology of the ruling class justified the suppression of others. For Marx the Christian faith was such an ideology. Christianity was part of a capitalist system which used belief in God to perpetuate itself.

Already with Lenin things changed. Lenin labeled communism (or socialism) *itself* an ideology. Communism had to be forged into a weapon in the most critical struggle in the world: the class struggle. This conflict demanded not just economic means, such as strikes or violence. It also required that the *consciousness* of the working class be directed ideologically to the one great ideal: the overthrow of the existing social order and the establishment of a new society based on the communal ownership of the means of production. The element of the human will to achieve the communist goal played a much more important role for Lenin than it did for Marx. Marx saw the revolution as the closure of an internal development within capitalism toward self-annihilation. Lenin consciously sought to bring that annihilation about, and he considered every means to the end permissible. Lenin created a full-fledged ideology, complete with an antithesis between good (the proletariat) and evil (the bourgeoisie), which he appropriated from Marx. All evil in the world could be traced to capitalism.

The ideology also had its own morality:

We say: Morality is what serves to destroy the old exploiting society and to unite all the working people around the proletariat, which is building up a new, communist society.[4]

The Communists must be prepared to make every sacrifice, and, if necessary, even to resort to all sorts of cunning, schemes, and stratagems, to employ illegal methods, to evade and conceal the truth.[5]

Moreover, Lenin taught a doctrine of sacrifice, or sacrificial readiness, saying that the revolution is a time to wade through streams of blood. We hear in his statement an echo of what a half century earlier Dostoyevsky had put into the mouth of Raskolnikov, the protagonist of *Crime and Punishment:*

But if for the sake of his idea [the destruction of the present in the name of the future] such a man has to step over a corpse or wade through blood, he is, in my opinion, absolutely entitled, in accordance with the dictates of his conscience, to permit himself to wade through blood, all depending of course on the nature and scale of the idea.[6]

But the goal of revolution requires *means* for its realization, even in Russia. Simply transforming morality to class morality, nar-towing love to class solidarity, and requiring of all art and science that they be partisan, that they side with the workers in the class struggle, were not sufficient. Lenin therefore called into existence technological, economic and political means to carry out the revolution and bring it to completion.

What has happened with these means? Under Khrushchev war was rejected as a means for solving disputes between states: "In its simplest expression [the policy of peaceful coexistence] signifies the repudiation of war as a means of solving controversial issues."[7] The class struggle must be carried forward on the economic plane, the technological plane, the plane of guerrilla and related forms of activity, and on the plane of ideology: "The main thing is to keep to the positions of ideological struggle, without resorting to arms in order to prove that one is right."[8] This broad class struggle requires means: a rapidly expanding production apparatus, constant research and development, a monitored educational system, an unrestricted propaganda program and a political and military apparatus. In 1961 the Communist Party Program of the Soviet Union described communism as follows:

Communism is a classless social system with one single form of public ownership of the means of production and full social equality of all members of society; under it, the all-round development of people will be accompanied by the growth of the productive forces through continuous progress in science and technology; all the springs of collective wealth will flow more abundantly, and the great principle "From each according to his ability, to each according to his needs" will be implemented.[9]

Technology, science, the forces of production: all are necessary and all must be mobilized.

But means so chosen and so distorted have religious significance. Though ostensibly they may be controlled by a more and more complex central planning bureau, in fact it is the path of these means which the Russians have followed over the course of time. They consider the means so indispensable that nothing prevents them from taking charge. The Soviet state, originally considered a temporary, limited catalyst in the transition phase from socialism to communism, has gradually become an awesome bureaucracy. The state has become a self-willed power, and its violence is persistent. It towers over the Russians as a god. The bureaucracy tyrannizes, and the revolution slays its own children.

The Soviet Union is a lesson in ideology from our own history. An ideology which is goal crazed awakens forces which people cannot control. Marx himself not only predicted the death of the state but passionately *desired* it. The end of the state signaled the end of capitalism! But in the communist block the reverse has taken place. In his book *The Alternative in Eastern Europe* Rudolf Bahro describes in somber details how the state has become a mute power, how the labor party has turned into a mere extension of that state and how the earlier feudal-agrarian despots have merely been replaced by industrial despots:

"Plan together, work together, govern together!" echoes the slogan from the loudspeakers, meaning that everyone is to show more system-conforming activity in his due place. But as soon as anyone ventures to overstep the limits of the prevailing regulations and institutions, he invariably hears the real message of the government: "Cobbler, stick to your last."[10]

Elsewhere in his book Bahro draws the conclusion: "The historical course of the Soviet Union [has been] a subjective and moral tragedy for all communists who can be taken seriously at the human level."[11] Bitterly he adds:

In the year 1900 Lenin expected the impending people's revolution "to sweep all bestiality from the Russian soil." Instead of this, the tremendous progress of the Soviet Union stands

comparison, in the most terrible way, with the "hideous pagan idol" invoked by Marx, who "would not drink the nectar but from the skulls of the slain."[12]
A dictatorial state which tyrannizes everything and everyone, even its highest officials (to prevent a coup)—how far we have come from Marx's dreams and "scientific" predictions! The revolution ideology *in action* inevitably creates an idol, the state, which is considered essential for regulating the economic system and for underwriting the economic and technological growth which will usher in communism. To that goal—the arrival of communism—everyone and everything must adapt. Once the ideology is set in motion, there is no turning back. The ideology calls forth *idols* (displaying its own form of religious incarnation) and commissions its *disciples,* who become its slaves.

The Lesson for Us
The communist ideology has all the trademarks of an ideology. An obsession with an end is evident in the glorification of the revolutionary pathos. The ideology venerates its own saints, the first revolutionaries, although it trusts that they will never return from the dead. Consistently it embraces any and every means—scientific, economic, technological and political—to reach its goals. As a result it respects no external norms. It twists God-given norms and mandates into partisan, class-determined norms and mandates until they become instruments in the class struggle. Did not Lenin say that truth comes out of the mouth of a rifle? The ideology uses even racial tensions to intensify the class struggle, and it demands the continual adaptation of people and the environment to the means to the end. Moreover, it carefully erects a false image of the enemy, capitalism and its henchmen, who bear the blame for all distress and exploitation. The criterion for the image is not truth but the goal.

The communist ideology is therefore a false revelation of sin and salvation. The working class carries the image of the suffering Messiah—including his sinlessness. The house of bondage which the exodus of communism leaves behind is capitalism. The full arrival of communism will be the incarnation of salvation. It is no wonder then that sacrifices must be offered, even the sacrifice of human blood, in order to make this redemption a reality. All the major elements of Christianity are therefore present, but in the form of idol worship.

The revelation offered by the revolution ideology makes the ideology a seductive power wherever people experience oppression and exploitation and desire liberation from their chains and misery. Like the communists, people may blame their suffering on the fact that they work for slave wages, and from there proceed to build up an ideology of liberation. Or they may use deep sexual or racial discrimination as a platform for pursuing self-preservation at any cost, and from there proceed to reinterpret humanity, sin, salvation, the meaning of life, society and the norms which apply to them. An ideology can anchor itself in the reality of any genuine threat, oppression and discrimination. Though the ideology gives life new substance, it also victimizes its adherents.

The revolution ideology is therefore seductively close to all of us. When we believe that resistance is our duty and that in order to resist we must create a morality and legality different from those we submit to in everyday life, then a destructive ideology is at work. Then, for example, no room exists for rejecting brutal means of violence. The ideology compels us to make new distinctions among means, so that good and evil no longer apply to everyone, including ourselves. Instead, good resides in those who are in "solidarity," and evil lies in the "opponents" of the cause. The process is set in motion whereby the means and methods unwittingly slip out of our control, sometimes mercilessly striking the first opponents of the resistance. Some liberation movements in the world—the Palestinian Liberation Organization, for example—have already traveled far down this ominous path, a path far removed from their original intention. In certain situations this deviation is certainly understandable; in the reality of the situation it is difficult to exercise restraint and to keep goals in proportion. But still it must be said that in some instances the revolution ideology has become the master of the movement. For when resistance grows into a distorting and self-legitimating ideology, the powers which the ideology awakens slip out of people's reach.

Oppression and violence take place in our society too. Violence and counterviolence meet in the streets—in Miami, Liverpool, Berlin, Beirut, Amsterdam, New York. Would this violence get so out of hand if ideologies were not at work? I do not believe so. If deep injustice creates an end which becomes all-embracing and which gains supporters, then sooner or later the end justifies any means. Those too who in a democratic society must restore the public order can easily fall into the temptation to make "an eye for an eye" the only valid law. Fortunately in North America this mistake is warned against: it is not worthy of the law state. Yet certain forces in our society do succumb to the temptation. Judges, police, or prison officials may be so distressed by disturbances within the public order that they consider past means inadequate and use other "tools" to bring the disorderly in line. If they defend these tools against any and every criticism, then a genuine, self-legitimating ideology has arisen. Such reactions contribute to the spiral of violence, a spiral which pulls both sides into itself.

The revolution ideology, an ideology of violence, therefore stands closer to us than we first thought. It is a temptation for both the left wing and the right wing, for those who passionately resist injustice and those who passionately defend authority. As an ideology it works its way into the most theologically orthodox right-wing circles, where sometimes upright politicians are humiliated and ostracized if they speak against the sacred party line.

CHAPTER 4

The Ideology of Nation

IDEOLOGIES DO NOT ARISE ACCIDENTALLY. THEY NEED DEEP injustice or threat to take hold. The ideology of nation, which aims for the preservation of a people's identity, is a case in point. For example, after the First World War Hitler used and misused the deep feelings of frustration and injury of the German people to assure the success of his National Socialist ideology. Without a previous history of wounded pride, the German people would not have embraced fascism so enthusiastically. In similar fashion the fascist dictators in South America today appeal to past national resentment to unite the masses of their corrupt regimes. The collective unconscious of a people harbors motives which can be and often are misused.

The nationalist ideology makes huge gains when a religious

element is added to it. One of the original emblems of fascism ac-
knowledges a close link between nation and religion: a bundle of
arrows (fasces) is linked to a whole in which the symbols of the
church and the state stand at the center. This false link between
the church and the state is typical of most nationalist ideologies.
The clergy and military work hand in hand to create national
unity. "One people, one nation, one leader," said Hitler. The
leadership stands against the equality of the people, autocracy
resists democracy, and compassion and peacemaking are mocked
as forms of weakness and cowardice. Sometimes a prominent military leadership tolerates and uses the church, as in Mussolini's
Italy and in some of the military regimes in South America. Or
the religious leadership may be dominant, as in the early Middle
Ages and as, in its own way, in Iran today.

We shall study the rise and activity of the nationalist ideology
with South Africa as our example. In South Africa unique elements come into play. The religious aspect, a distinct kind of
Calvinism, is certainly present. But nationalism in South Africa
today cannot be explained by the dominance of either the church
or political leadership. The origins of "apartheid" and "separate
development" lie much deeper. It is because of those origins that
I choose South Africa. For we must realize that under similar circumstances any nation which claims a Christian origin can fall
into the trap of a nationalist ideology.

A Threatened People

The history of the white Afrikaners has always been one of
fundamental threat to their people. The "Great Trek" north in
the 1830s, which James Michener traces through the eyes of the
Van Doorn family in *The Covenant*,[1] was not a sort of political
tour de force. It was a real flight from the harsh surroundings
of English colonialism. The threat was even greater during the

Boer War (1899-1902). The first concentration camps in history were built on African, not German soil. During and after the war more Afrikaners were killed in British concentration camps than in the battles themselves. The camps claimed the lives of 26,000 men, women and children.

In such circumstances it is understandable that maintaining a people's identity, including its language, culture, freedoms and rights, takes on an enormous, even all-encompassing significance. It is understandable too that these strong Calvinists came to believe in a direct covenant between themselves and God. On December 16, 1838, during the Great Trek, the Afrikaners fought a decisive battle at the Blood River. Though three thousand Zulu warriors died, the Afrikaners sustained only three injuries and no deaths. They saw their victory as the sign of a new covenant, the beginning of a new exodus and the establishment of a new, God-given freedom. Though they suffered, eventually they found deliverance in the formation of a "Christian nation." If you stand in front of the mammoth pioneer monument outside of Pretoria, where the words *Ons vir jou Suid Afrika* ["We are for you, South Africa"] are engraved in granite, you feel something of the single-minded will of the Afrikaner people to preserve their identity at any price. At stake is the oath of the early Afrikaners to build a Christian nation, an oath for which many sacrificed their lives.

But the protection of the Afrikaner nation and identity requires means. In the multiracial society of South Africa, where the whites form a clear minority, complex legal and political measures are needed to protect the uniqueness of the Afrikaner Christian nation. Also needed is a strong security force to enforce order and to quell mounting opposition. In the need for these means lies the origin of the apartheid policy, which was later translated into the more dynamic policy of "separate development" for the different peoples within South Africa.

Apartheid is a policy which in practice flouts the most elementary norms of justice and love. It legalizes a detailed and highly intricate system of discrimination among subjects of the state based solely on differences in skin color. The whites have far more rights than the blacks or the coloreds. The homeland policy, the "great apartheid," gives racial discrimination its formal, legal basis, allowing the government both to make economic use of the many black workers and to relegate their political rights and cultural identity to the homelands. Politically speaking, blacks and coloreds are treated as subjects of political bodies other than the Republic of South Africa. This treatment is also given to the "urban blacks," who have never seen their own so-called homeland, though they were born on South African soil. Nonwhites are economically desirable "labor units" and politically undesirable aliens. They are not full human beings welcome in the land of their birth.

Ideological Justice and Love
How does the white Christian Afrikaner wash his or her hands of such deep injustice? Even the Old Testament sojourner laws were more humane than the laws for South Africa's own black residents. Have not the Afrikaners' means of power become so distorted that they simply do not square with the basic principles of the law state?

South Africa demonstrates the strength of a genuine ideology. The Afrikaner ideology bends and reinterprets the requirements of justice and love to such an extent that these mandates not only fail to resist the goal of national insulation but actually support it. It illustrates that the Bible can be read so selectively that it becomes a handbook for the protection of a people's uniqueness at any cost.

When questioned about justice, South Africans often point to
former Dutch Prime Minister Abraham Kuyper's distinction between nation and state.[2] They point out that for Kuyper the nation or people was "organic." It sprang from nature and therefore fell under the original will of the Creator. The state, by contrast, was mechanical and artificial. Kuyper believed that the
organic had priority over the mechanical.

Kuyper's distinction generates a specific result when applied
to the "multiracial" society of South Africa. Afrikaners argue that
the existence of different peoples has priority over the existence
of the state. The state must therefore yield to the will of a people
to preserve its identity. Consequently, Afrikaners claim that justice for and within the Afrikaner people has precedence over the
"revolutionary demand" for equal justice among all citizens of
the state. It should be clear then that Afrikaners view certain
forms of "necessary" discrimination between blacks and whites
as forms of justice. For one people is of course not another.
Each has its own legal history, culture and stage or degree of
civilization. National differences supersede the principle that one
must treat all subjects of the state "on the same footing," a tenet
of the law state. Different things must be treated differently,
and differences between peoples and races must be acknowl-
edged within the realm of justice.

With respect to love, similar principles hold. Not long ago in
South Africa I asked an Afrikaner New Testament scholar what
it means to love our neighbor as ourselves. In all sincerity he
answered that the command to love our neighbor means indeed
that we love our neighbor, even our black neighbor, as ourselves.
But he added two qualifications. In the first place, the command-
ment leaves room for loving yourself, and therefore for yourself
as an Afrikaner. Jesus' words may not be interpreted, therefore,
as something which inhibits the protection of one's national iden-

tity. And in the second place, a certain order must be observed when you love your neighbor. First, you must love Christians of your own people. Second, you must love Christians who do not belong to your people. Third, you must love members of your people who are not believers. And fourth, you must love non-Christians of other peoples.

All in all, this view of love carries the trademarks of an ideology. It is miles away from the agape love which Jesus taught us to have, an unconditional love which crosses all boundaries of nation and class. The answer to the question: Who is my neighbor? comes from the gospel itself. My neighbor is *whoever* asks for my help, like the victim of robbers whom the Samaritan—the black South African of Jesus' day—loved and cared for.

National Religion and the Enemy

More in South Africa points to the presence of a genuine nationalist ideology. A close tie exists between a powerful church and a powerful state, as in the original fascism. The church functions as an uncritical support for the occasionally brutal state. The Dutch Reformed Church has been called the "National Party at prayer." Nationalist ideology is apparent even in the symbol of the pioneer monument: it is an empty temple, five stories high, set on a high hill overlooking Pretoria. On the walls inside, a mural of painted wagons arranged in a circle (the *laager,* an Afrikaner symbol of strength) retells the entire history of the Afrikaner people. Every year on the Day of the Covenant, December 16, at noon, a tiny hole in the dome allows a stream of light to fall precisely on the letter *o* in *Ons vir* jou *Suid Afrika.* Many children are baptized at the monument on the Day of the Covenant. The unanswered question is whether any people or nation may claim such absolute devotion of its subjects to its own national existence.

The South African government carefully paints its picture

of the enemy and the traitor. Any form of opposition to the existing regime and its discriminatory and humanly degrading laws—
I think of the Immorality Act, the classification of children from
mixed marriages by skin color, the Relocation Policy, the Bantu
Education Act, which for economic purposes restricts education
opportunities for the blacks, and the forced separation of married couples, in which the wife is forbidden to live with her hus-
band—any opposition to these is automatically seen as communist. Political prisoners are numerous, and victims, such as
Stephen Biko, are present too. The fact that the communist
ideology spreads *because* of the government's policies seldom or
never gets through to the Afrikaners.

What strikes one in South Africa is how the means of an ideology take on their own sinister strength and expand into vicious
powers. The apartheid legislation is more and more difficult to
maintain. Increasingly it leads to unscrupulous injustice and
brushes harder against the grain of reality. Even police sym-
pathetic to the government find the laws hard to put into effect.
But the legislation *does* exist, and an enormously bureaucratic
government, police and military oversee its further implementation and application. Any significant deviation from the ideology
of "separate development" can land you in the traitor's cell.
Those like Donald Woods or Beyers Naudé, whose greatest sin
is that they struggle against the apartheid ideology with no other
weapon than words, suffer under years of house arrest or ban-
ishment.

The Afrikaner ideology is deeply unbiblical. It is based on a
fusion of Calvinism and fascism. Did not an architect of apartheid
list the Nazi slogan "blood and soil" next to "faith" and "culture"
as a trademark of Afrikanerdom in the forties? Surely, the desire
to protect life as a people is understandable in principle, and
even legitimate. But the absolutization of that desire leads to the

ruin of the entire South African population. Because of that absolutization, white South Africa adds daily to the huge pile of sins which already have been committed against South Africa's black population. "Whoever wants to save his life will lose it, but whoever loses his life for me will find it," we read in the Gospels.[3] The future of South Africa will be determined by no other law. An act of penance toward the black population, which results in an offer to the black leaders to pull their chairs around the decision-making table of the whites, is the only real way out. Four visits to South Africa in recent years have brought me to that firm conviction.[4]

The Lesson for Us
Within South Africa the five trademarks of a full-fledged ideology are present. It is therefore a complete ideology—although not yet absolute, as the continuing struggle between the "hardline" *(verkramptes)* and "enlightened" *(verligtes)* nationalists testifies (a battle waged entirely within the framework of the nationalist ideology). But more importantly, the history of South Africa demonstrates that Christians can fall fully for an ideology of nation. Even orthodox doctrine is an insufficient antidote for it. The danger of the nationalist ideology exists in both Catholic and Protestant countries, which raises the question of whether we in the West fare any better than those in South Africa.

At the center of the ideology of nation arise questions about how we treat our own cultural and racial minorities: blacks, Hispanics, native peoples and migrant workers. In the course of the coming years these questions will only intensify. Policy and practice already show that these minorities upset us, and we fear for our future. Racial discrimination is again on the rise. The Ku Klux Klan is flourishing, both in the United States and Canada. What will the United States do as blacks and Hispanics become

stronger and more vocal? Or what will Canada do as energy proj-
ects increasingly threaten the native peoples' way of life? Are we
ready to give these minorities equal civil rights? Or will our desire
to protect our identity push us to apply somewhat different legislation to them? The recent hesitation of the Reagan administra-
tion to extend the Voting Rights Act of 1965 and the approval of
the new Canadian constitution, which makes little provision for
native peoples, may suggest the latter.

But the temptation to link up with a fascist ideology is even
greater. Today, as violence increases and the economic upheaval
gets worse, voices reminiscent of those in Germany in the thirties
cry for a strong leader to restore law and order, reinstate full
economic liberty and make America great again by means of legislation, the media and a strong security force. For is not communism on the rise everywhere? These cries certainly carry some
ideological traits. If the main interest of policy is to preserve
the greatness and superiority of America,[5] if love is equated with
love for America, and if American interests determine what is
"good" and "just,"[6] then a nationalist ideology—a civil religion—
is at work. If a national flag is honored as the expression of what
gives life ultimate meaning, it can become a symbol of idolatry.

During difficult times democracy falters, and the national urge
for a strong leader returns. That was the real problem in the
thirties. Movements like National Socialism *do* repeat themselves,
and an undercurrent in our population, especially in orthodox
right-wing circles, lends the temptation a certain credibility. It is
a pitfall in which the cures will be worse than the illness, and the
means for maintaining order will slip out of control. And then
it will be too late.

But the nationalist ideology is even closer to us than this. The
heart of it, the decision to protect your national identity at any
expense, touches more than just national unity. The goal of self-

preservation can infiltrate any human group or organization. The ideology can be cherished by ostracized groups of people, political parties, businesses or even churches which strongly desire to protect their identities. The opportunity for pursuing the nationalist ideology therefore lies extremely close to home. We all belong to various social, political, religious and racial groupings. Feelings of threat, superiority or pride can creep into them at any time. When they do, we may nurture an attitude which seeks to protect our identity by distinguishing ourselves from other human beings. We may, for example, use the assumed "inferiority" of being poor, black, non-Christian or uneducated as a demonic instrument for assuring the "superiority" of being rich, white, Christian or educated.

So much suffering on this earth has its root in this ideological distortion! How else can we explain the many persecutions of Jews throughout history, especially in the midst of so-called Christian nations and communities? How else can we explain the permanent state of misery for the world's most desperately poor? The rich "need" the poor to glorify their own self-esteem. In a manner of speaking, through this ideological distortion Christ is crucified again—Christ, the impoverished Jew who was despised and rejected by the ruling religious elite of his time.

So the ideology of national or group identity lies within reach of us all. Even the goal of defending authority can expand into a dangerous ideology, not just in South Africa, but in North America too.[7]

CHAPTER 5

The Ideology of Material Prosperity

WE ALL KNOW THAT THE RACE FOR MONEY AND MATERIAL POS-
sessions is deeply entrenched. Selfish emotions often flare up
when the issue of dividing wealth arises.

But is it legitimate to ask whether the pursuit of material
prosperity in our society carries the trademarks of an ideology?
Several developments suggest that it is.

Disappointing Progress

First it must be said that the current prosperity of the majority
of us was completely lacking only a few decades ago. If we go back
in Western history one hundred years, we find terrible poverty
and an alarmingly high death rate—just as in the developing
countries today. Unbelievably long workdays at starvation wages,

and overcrowded, pitiful shanties were common. Often our grandparents, and perhaps even our parents, led beggars' lives. My own father never went beyond elementary school because my grandparents could not afford more tuition. A principal offered to foot the bill for his education, but with sorrow my grandparents refused: the wage which the young boy earned kept the family from losing its balance on the edge of existence.

Our society had to find a way of escape. Under these conditions the struggle against economic misery became a strong motivator, and the industrial system was accepted as the panacea. Sometimes industry was hard and dehumanizing, and it created great social inequality. But at the end of the long tunnel flickered the daylight, namely, liberation from their awful poverty.

The circumstances of life have drastically improved since then. Can we also say that we have entered the daylight? Fifty years ago in an essay entitled "The Economic Possibilities for Our Grandchildren," the English economist John Maynard Keynes wrote that the daylight had indeed arrived.[1] The system of production had already reached a substantial capacity, and the age of a flood of consumable goods and of considerably more leisure time was upon us. Prosperity was around the corner. Was Keynes right? Certainly the wave of consumer products has washed over us, but when our thoughts turn to genuine human well-being, we often think of yesterday, not today. The shrinkage of work hours continues, but often it reaches us in the form of higher unemployment. Keynes was wrong. The tunnel is still here, albeit a little higher and wider. And many see no daylight flickering at its end. Instead, they feel a sort of intangible threat.

The very progress which we first applauded has now become a problem. It seems that economic progress stimulates inflation, risky energy development, higher accumulations of toxic wastes underground and in the atmosphere, deforestation[2] and an unbelievable arms race, which already absorbs 5 to 15 per cent of the scarce raw materials of the world.[3] The production system, initially a willing servant laboring to end our misery, seems to have taken charge. Through its demands for economic growth and rising productivity it tells all of us, whether management or labor, what limits to place on protecting the environment, how many jobs to eliminate, what kind of workers are no longer suitable in the labor system, and what products and necessities must be consumed. And usually we simply *listen,* for, so the argument goes, how can we overtake growing unemployment without continuous economic growth?

A major reason for pursuing economic growth is that without such growth the government loses the basis for its necessary expenditures. This threatens our whole system of social security, which then makes the need for economic growth seem more acute. The deficits of government have already risen to fantastic ranges, and it appears that these deficits can be eliminated only through a vigorous recuperation of our economic production. But suppose that growth returns even on a moderate scale; will we recover like before? Fear that we will *not* has become a part of the threat of the future—as remarkable as that phrase may sound. For fulfilling our critical short-term needs contributes to our long-term threat: pollution in the atmosphere and in the ground, and the depletion of raw materials and energy.[4]

These developments do indeed suggest the presence of an ideology. As we have seen, adjustment to means is a trademark of an ideology in action. And clearly here the goal of material prosperity requires us to adjust our behavior to its means—continuous economic growth. We have become dependent on economic growth, and it has ensnared us. Though initially a relatively innocent tool, it has become established as a power against us. It coerces us and reveals to us what we must do to survive.

Probably for these reasons economic growth no longer has a halo around it. Much of its earlier allure is lost. But its rigidity is intact. The question now is survival. Our backs are to the wall, and our ability simply to maintain what we have already acquired is at stake. Our attitude toward economic growth is this: moderation, if necessary. Zero growth: only as a last resort. Taking a step backward: *never*.

But we have not yet completed the picture of a full-fledged ideology. The goal, material prosperity, certainly exists, and many groups in our society have dug in their heels to achieve it. The means exist too: technology, economic organization, production capacity and economic policy. With respect to what they may do to humans and the environment, these means are certainly not scrutinized by the biblical standards of stewardship. But what about the commands to do justice and to love our neighbor? *Their* redefinition is what betrays an ideology.

The Rise of the Welfare State

Recently a variety of comments have been made about the rise and organization of the welfare state. For in the last few decades the welfare state has undergone a striking development.

Until the Second World War politicians viewed the state as a law state. The state was seen as the institution necessary for protecting the rights of its citizens: the rights of free expression, worship and property. Around World War 2, however, that view enlarged. Material welfare in society as a whole had increased. This gave government the possibility of expanding its legal concern for society toward the financially weak. Government created a system of social guarantees, beginning with Franklin Roosevelt's Social Security Act of 1935. This enlargement was certainly a positive development! It fit entirely within the framework of a genuine law state, a state which promotes justice in more than a formal sense.

But the story does not end there. Economic growth kept rising, and as it rose so rose the persuasiveness of arguments by people who thought they deserved a bigger piece of the pie. It is important to see that they formulated their demands as *rights,* as the right to government aid, the right to housing, the right to part of the wealth, the right to work. Their demands were addressed directly to the government, which through its policies guaranteed those rights.

Economic rights are naturally different from the rights ordinarily granted by the law state. Rights of *acquisition* were added to the earlier rights of *protection,* and soon they demanded most of the government's attention. As rights to parts of the growing abundance, they presupposed that a growth in economic prosperity would continue.

This shift altered the norm of social justice. At its origin, justice calls us to attend to people in need—widows, orphans, the handicapped, aliens, and others weak and abandoned—so that they may be restored as whole persons in society. The new rights of acquisition distorted this norm in a twofold manner. First, social justice for the aged and the unemployed became primarily or exclusively a question of adequate *financial* payment. People in need received an economic or monetary allowance. The weak were economically protected, and this protection was seen as sufficient. Money could do the job, irrespective of the causes of their position. Second, the meaning of justice became increasingly dynamic. Every group, weak or strong, soon believed that it held a natural right to a larger slice of an ever-larger economic pie.[5] An unwritten law stated that no one could fall behind. The consequence of this double distortion was a demand for more economic growth regardless of the obstacles. Through the heavy accent on necessary economic growth, the norm of social justice became an instrument for constantly increasing our material abundance.

Justice today has therefore lost its edge. An essential part of true justice is that often it is critical of continuous economic expansion. When people are sidestepped in the production process, or when meaning is taken out of the work process for either labor or management, then the norm of social justice is violated. We identify these casualties as sacrifices for the sake of progress. We believe that people should be happy when we give them financial compensation. But financial compensation is not justice; it is often the defacement of justice in the midst of a materialistic society.

Similarly, the command to love our neighbor has lost its force. We look first for the economic translation of the norm instead of exploring the real signs of misery, loneliness and discrimination. Love has become a matter of money, a matter for professional or bureaucratic attention. Solidarity has become an act of the government.

The Teetering Welfare State
The distortion of justice is evident in the consequences. New groups of the deprived and neglected have arisen. We find them in those who receive unemployment benefits, in the unemployed youth, in the assembly-line workers, in the unemployed white-collar workers, in the drug addicts and in the deeply lonely of our society. What course of action do these people take—if they have any strength left? They make rigorous financial demands. How else can they tangibly express their feeling of discrimination? A scream no longer gets them real attention or genuine justice. They speak the language which is the most impressive and effective means of communication in a society overly sensi-

tive to money and material prosperity. And their claims are directed mainly to the government. Is not the government there for the common good? And like an overworked vending machine, which can give out only what is put in, government works frantically to meet the demands: expenditures, subsidies and loans.

This pattern cannot go on forever. For what will happen as economic growth retards and as taxes bring in less and less income because of growing resistance to paying taxes (a new taxation morality which also has ideological roots)? Actually government currently finds itself in this position. And because our greedy society does not often put on the harness of restraint, government reaches for the only means at its disposal: an increase in budget deficits. Increased deficits push it to artificially increase the money supply, because then government can pay out more than it takes in. But this medicine hardly cures the ailment. It only intensifies it. Extra money means more inflation and more unemployment, the people who are the weakest are ostracized even more, and government deficits rise again.

In our time it seems that we approach the point where the "government aid" rights of various elements in the population teeter—and with them the welfare state itself. Should the recovery of economic growth not happen, as we may expect, those assistance rights will sound hollow. They simply will no longer be guaranteed, as we see already in countries like The Netherlands and Belgium. As rights of *acquisition* they depend on constantly growing economic prosperity, and hence they are only as durable as the growth in prosperity itself.

The imminent end of the welfare state is no trifling matter. It will create a deep crisis of trust in our society as a whole, a crisis putting democracy itself in danger. In all likelihood people will repay the infringement of their "rights" with bitter accusations against politicians, whose constant promises, sealed in law, cannot be kept. In that "hour of truth" politicians will feel inclined to postpone the painful outcome for as long as possible. The impulse then to heighten deficits will be even more irresistible until government finances are thrown totally out of gear. If that path is taken—the way of delay—then we must fear for the continued existence of our democratic law state.

Already today our whole society founders, having snagged itself on an obsession with continuous economic progress. It has refused to understand the signs of the times. In the idiom of this book I can state this somewhat differently: our own gods have betrayed us just when we needed them most. Let us be honest: our attitude toward the welfare state is a *religious matter*. To many people and institutions it is a god, to which you may put your request and from which you may expect everything: your work, your housing and your economic security. But this god fails us precisely at the critical moment, when the expectations reach their climax. The ritual around the welfare state today is a ritual around a hollow idol, officiated by a priesthood of politicians.

An Incomplete Ideology

Not all ideologies are complete, and not all their adherents give them the opportunity to wreak the havoc of chaos, terror and horror caused by the ideology of Marxism/Leninism in Stalinist Russia, the fascist ideologies of Hitler in Germany and Mussolini in Italy, and the rigid nationalist ideologies in some Latin American countries today.

The welfare ideology is an example of an incomplete ideology. Not all our society's organizations—labor unions, businesses, political parties and so forth—labor under the curse of maintaining prosperity at any cost. God's commands of justice and love are not entirely tainted by the prosperity ideology. Certain limits on what economic progress may inflict on people and the environment are still respected. The artificial enemy, another characteristic of the full-fledged ideology, exists to some extent (I think of the ease with which some very legitimate criticisms of our production system are brushed aside as "socialist" or "leftist," while other criticisms of the welfare state are dismissed as "rightist"), but the image is not as finely articulated as in other ideologies.

But my nuancing at this point should not suggest that the prosperity ideology will not run its course. Though the trademarks of the prosperity ideology are relatively weak, the scope of the ideology is alarmingly wide. It spreads to the remotest developing country and leaves behind irreparably deep footprints. It has aroused economic, political, technological and scientific powers which to a great degree are autonomous and self-governing. Their dictates have been woven deep into the fabric of our society. The ideology claims both multinational corporations and supranational organizations such as the European Economic Community, whose first priority is furthering the material welfare of its member states,[6] and international growth-oriented bodies like the Organization for Economic Cooperation and Development[7] and the International Monetary Fund. The enormous power of these and other international and transnational institutions and bodies steadily increases. Economically and technologically they *never* listen to the word *enough,* and they expand into the broadest international relationships. The adjustment which they require of government policy and behavior, of people and of the environment is staggering.

We also must not forget that a committed prosperity ideology influences more than just someone's physical or material circumstances. It causes the boundaries which restrict permissible violence and aggression in human relationships to widen or gradually disappear. That disappearance is to be expected in a society where the meaning of life is given over to its own economic goals. The more forcefully existing standards stress what "must" take place for the sake of progress, the more other "weaker" standards fade into the background. "Ultimate ends" (goals which flow from what groups of people and societies ultimately want to reach) sooner or later replace true norms. Nihilism attacks whatever forms a barrier to life here and now. In many places abortion, for example, is judged less by biblical norms than by the contribution it can make to making life easier and to solving the overpopulation problem (this is especially true in Japan). Abortion legislation has shifted from the sphere of rights of protection to the sphere of rights of acquisition. "No God, no master" was not just the slogan of the French Revolution: it accompanies every declaration of human autonomy and every submission to other norms. The number of abortions in Russia is four abortions to every child born; of five possible children from one mother, only one survives. Is that in store for our society too?

A Crossroads
At the level of the prosperity ideology our society has arrived at a junction. Economic growth has dwindled (a more detailed explanation of why follows in chapter 7). Many rights taken for granted earlier, including the rights of acquisition, now rest on shaky ground. Growing numbers protest specific forms of technological progress, such as nuclear energy, and the use of new scientific breakthroughs, such as the discoveries of bioengineering (the technique of interfering with human genetic properties). These are signs that our society has arrived at a crossroads.

What will we do at the crossroads? If we embrace all forms of technological and economic progress and at the same time curtail foreign aid, remove all environmental restrictions, submit to the blackmail of the oil producing countries and accept weapons from wherever they come—all for the sake of maintaining and expanding our economic achievements—then the prosperity ideology will certainly become full-fledged and absolute.

This ideology will then put in place a new and rigid image of the enemy. Our energy suppliers will become our friends and, consequently, Israel will become our enemy. The ideology will use tyrannical measures against all who resist new and seemingly necessary technologies. It will consistently give preference to the employed over the unemployed and will show little concern for the environment and for the world's weakest countries.

The new ideology will also give birth to a society where the government will surrender to illegitimate pressure. The law state will wilt because of strong economic pressure groups. It will be replaced either by a *consensus state* (joint rule by the government and by the most powerful economic pressure groups) or by an enlightened dictator, who will be considered necessary to bring rebellious interest groups in line. Within this framework an infinite toleration will grow for aggressive persons and groups, as long as their actions do not interfere with economic or technological progress. An ideological society can tolerate personal ruin. It can sympathize with it. It gives its inhabitants permissiveness, not justice. It practices toleration instead of love.

Am I too pessimistic? Perhaps I am. But a genuine ideology has no flexibility. It has the tendency to drive people to the extreme.

CHAPTER 6

The Ideology of Guaranteed Security

DEFENDING A COUNTRY AGAINST POSSIBLE ATTACK IS NOT JUST a legitimate goal. In times of real threat it can be a moral and political duty. In the thirties, for example, Dutch defense efforts were virtually absent, even though the militarist Nazis in Germany had accumulated vast power and had publicly declared their intention to expand German territory. The Dutch people were also spiritually unprepared for what brewed across their border. Many people, including Christians, claimed that Hitler had merely restored authority in Germany with a strong arm and simply wanted to take up the gauntlet against onrushing world communism. The right wing minimized the significance of protecting Holland by dismissing the dangers of the rising fascism; the left wing did the same by advocating total pacifism. The

Netherlands entered the Second World War spiritually and militarily unprepared.

The devastation, suffering and resistance of those war years are etched indelibly on the memories of many in North America and Europe today. Repeatedly, they say "never again." In doing so they often transfer the situation of World War 2 to today, simply putting new names to the old faces. They equate the Nazism of then with the Russian communism of now, and they identify the pacifists of then with those who support various church peace movements today. The picture seems to fit. For does not communism, an ideology of revolution, seek to control the world, just as National Socialism did? They argue that the threat of communism requires us to pay increasing attention to defense in order to maintain the balance of power and to frighten the Russians from attacking us. And you may say of nuclear weapons what you will (so they argue), but in the last thirty years they have safeguarded peace and security in our part of the world.

Yet something is lacking in this picture. The balance of power —a phrase used even before World War 1—no longer has a fixed boundary or limit. It governs itself, and its momentum seems unbreakable. It breaks through every conceivable ceiling, even that of the total annihilation of the opponent. The facts are well-known: we now have sufficient weapons capacity to destroy the world more than thirty times (once would already seem superfluous). More destructive power is directed at every *city* in the East and West than the *total* amount of munition consumed in all of world history, including the two world wars.[1] In spite of this enormous and redundant power of destruction, America and Russia together build three to six new nuclear bombs a day, or more than one thousand a year. Is any restraint evident in these weapons developments? Or have weapons technology and the arms race held the world hostage, relentlessly imposing their will on us as an autonomous power?

These questions add ideology to the picture. We may not exclude the possibility that an ideology has worked its way into *our* thinking and behavior. Perhaps we have allowed means to go over our heads, and now they tower over us as gods.

War and Peace in History

To ascertain the presence of a security ideology we must begin far back in Western history. We do not understand our current strategic problems, in part, because we have lost a sense of history and lack insight into our past communal guilt.

How have people understood war and peace in the past? At least three historical developments stand out. The first is the rise of the Renaissance man more than five centuries ago. During the Renaissance, people wanted to unburden themselves from the yoke of the authoritarian medieval church and to create a new world. This would be achieved not only through new techniques in art, science and world exploration (Columbus's travels were a fruit of the new attitude) but also through a new method of warfare. Besides being a great artist and scientist, Leonardo da Vinci was the ingenious designer of new weapons of war, including a submarine and a helicopter. For him the style of war was one of the new "arts" of autonomous man, who through reason and intellect could force peace on his enemies. "O God, thou art willing to sell us everything at the price of our labor," was his prayer. About the same time, Machiavelli wrote his famous book *The Art of War*,[2] and in *The Prince* he wrote: "There cannot be good laws where there are not good arms; and where there are good arms there must be good laws."[3] Peace and prosperity for the Renaissance man were manufacturable; they were seen as potential results of man's own efforts.

During the period which followed (the sixteenth to the eighteenth century) a host of national wars were fought according to the new rules of the game. At first, wars were fought by mercenaries, but soon ordinary citizens bore arms.

During this period the Dutch jurist Hugo Grotius attempted to set certain limits to warfare. Using the principle of natural law, he justified armed defense and formulated guidelines to which all warfare should adhere. To warfare he fixed two main conditions: the purpose of any armed conflict must be peace; and people must limit the means. In any war situation, armies must spare women and children, abstain from cruelty and respect existing property. Reminiscent of the laws of Deuteronomy 20, Grotius's guidelines point to the enduring norms which the Creator of heaven and earth gave humankind for situations of conflict.

The second development occurred during the French Revolution. In 1793 the French National Convention issued a "mass conscription" *(leveé en masse)* proclamation, drafting the entire French population into the uprising against their oppressors. Men and women, young and old, were mobilized:

The National Convention, having heard the report of its Committee of Public Safety, decrees:

Article 1. From this moment until the time when the enemy is driven from the territory of the Republic, all Frenchmen are drafted into the service of the army.

Let the young men go into combat; the married men forge weapons and transport provisions; the women make army tents and uniforms and serve in the hospitals; the children tear up linen; and the elderly be put in public places in order to stir up the courage of the soldiers and preach the hatred of the kings and the unity of the Republic.[4]

The concept of total war, war using any and every means, was born.

The concept of total war was developed theoretically a half century later by the German Carl von Clausewitz.[5] For him war was a normal and indispensable instrument for achieving political ends. He described modern warfare as a conflict between nations in which a total deployment of all possibilities and forces is legitimate. Nations should commit to the struggle all their labor, their whole system of production, all their natural resources, their whole culture and all other means of assistance. Literature and art must promote victory, as must the news service and propaganda. The end justifies the means, because in war life and death itself is at stake.

The third feature of this history is the discovery in 1866 of dynamite or "security powder," as the inventor, Alfred Nobel called it. Nobel's invention stimulated an enormous expansion of the technology of warfare, thanks partly to the rapidly growing natural sciences.

What inspired Nobel to call his sinister invention "security powder"? Or what caused him to allot the vast sums of money which his weapons factory earned to the Nobel Peace Prize, which even today naive scientists and politicians cheerfully accept? Do not Nobel's actions suggest a form of schizophrenia?[6] Undoubtedly they do. But Nobel reconciled these impossible tensions in his life by maintaining that the expansion of the military's destructive possibilities would make peace on earth an incontrovertible fact. "I hope," he once wrote, "to discover a weapon so terrible that it would make war eternally impossible." Hence the invention of the security powder, and hence the financing of the Nobel Peace Prize with money made from weapons.

Eighty years later the first atomic bombs fell on Hiroshima and Nagasaki. Was that the fulfillment of Nobel's long-cherished dream?

The Lessons of the Past

This brief history suggests several things. First, already far back in history the waging of war and/or the defense of one's territory were seen as ends for which the normal rules and norms of justice do not hold. The end was too important or too decisive. A countermovement was begun by Hugo Grotius and later elaborated by jurists like Cornelius van Vollenhoven.[7] It led to a few international treaties and conventions, such as the Hague Peace Conference (1899 and 1907), which outlawed the bombardment of open cities, and the Geneva Conference of 1925, which declared that the development of chemical weapons violated international law. But it seems that these principles of justice, including the noninvolvement of the civilian population and of women and children, are a vague memory today. In a real conflict situation noncombatants may be erased entirely. The Nazis bombed Rotterdam (an open city), and the Allies bombarded the civilian population of Dresden. Conflict, menace and war write their own law: the law of the strongest. Today, with the possibility of using nuclear weapons, has it not become meaningless to speak of forbidding the killing of innocent women and children?

Second, long ago a reversal occurred in the order of how people thought about peace, security, justice and love. The biblical order has always been this: do justice, love your neighbor, respect the Torah, and then you will have life. In other words, seek first the kingdom of God and his righteousness, and all that remains —*including* peace and prosperity—will be added to you. Since the Renaissance, however, when peace became a product of human technique and science, the Western order has been this: put peace, security and prosperity first, and then freedom, equality, justice, brotherhood and sisterhood will be added to you as the harvest of your labors. Biblical norms are very nice, but they must not hinder human progress toward prosperity and peace.

Finally, building up technology in order to coerce peace increased the means of military destruction and the probability of their use. The increase was both in range and in depth. The circle of persons and areas of life involved in military conflict became larger (today it envelops all citizens and all sectors of life), and gradually modern weapons technology itself took control over the problem of war and peace. Weapons technology today is not restricted by the principles of international law. It is "restricted" only by the goal of protecting national interests at any cost. The schizophrenia of Alfred Nobel generated a split in all Western culture: more weapons (more *human* accomplishments) will create peace.

The Strategies of NATO

Let us now look at more recent history. In reality, more weapons threatened peace. In the years after World War 2 our civilization acquired full command of the technology of splitting the atom: an instrument for waging war and maintaining peace. Shortly after the erection of the North Atlantic Treaty Alliance (NATO) in 1948, the atom bomb was added to its arsenal. Paul Henri Spaak began his NATO inaugural address with the words, "We are all afraid." How would NATO, conceived in the reality of possible armed Soviet aggression and aware of the lessons of history, handle this new totalitarian weapon?

The first strategy of NATO was "massive retaliation" to a conventional attack by Russia. Some years later, however, Russia was believed to be approaching the production of nuclear weapons. Because of Russia's advancing technology, NATO developed a new strategy under the title "Mutually Assured Destruction" (MAD). From that point on Russia and America tacitly sought to hold each other's population hostage, as it were, in order to ward off the danger of a nuclear war. Each knew that after taking a first blow it needed to have enough remaining power to destroy a large segment of the opponent's civilian population. Each country needed "second strike capability." The United States in particular devoted itself to maintaining and building up this capacity. During this time (from 1948 until around 1970), something of Alfred Nobel's dream seemed to be realized. New weapons were available, weapons so terrible that war seemed an impossibility. Politicians began to view peace as the result of technology and science! For the *nonuse* of these means of destruction stood at the forefront. Presumably the arms race would end when that weapons ceiling was reached which would guarantee the total elimination of the enemy and its population in the event of a first strike. After that, more weapons would surely be unnecessary and senseless!

Around 1970 that ceiling was reached. One American nuclear submarine then had the capability to destroy 160 Russian cities simultaneously. Every nuclear submarine which survived a Soviet first strike could therefore accomplish the necessary total destruction. Consequently, a further increase of strategic weapons was no longer necessary. Sufficient deterrence had been reached *regardless* of whether the Soviet Union wanted to strategically arm itself further.

But the dismal story is that during the seventies the world staged a greater arms race than ever before. After 1970 both sides, the Soviet Union and NATO, multiplied their capacity to destroy the world ten times. The new MX missile system of the United States has a destructive force at least 10,000 times greater than the bomb dropped on Hiroshima, which killed 140,000 people. And annual weapons expenditures in the world as a whole are now higher than the gross national products of the poorest half of the world population.[8] Why did this development take place?

The Shift of 1969

In his recent memoirs, *The White House Years,* Henry Kissinger suggests why.[9] In 1969 Kissinger summoned the Chiefs of Staff to explain that the United States could not escape adjusting its strategy of Mutually Assured Destruction. Armaments and weapons technology in the East and West had advanced to such a stage that strategic nuclear weapons could now be aimed more and more both at *tactical* targets—that is, on the battlefield—and also directly at well-defined *military* targets, such as missile silos. Kissinger wanted to create room for this realignment in American strategy, particularly to lessen the chances of a total eradication of the American population in case of a general conflict.

This was a moment of tremendous significance. The reasoning of Kissinger consisted of a proposal to break through the existing weapons ceiling. No longer were we to view strategic weapons as weapons whose *nonuse* is primary at all times. On a limited scale these weapons could be deployed, if necessary, against military targets to prevent more serious destruction. Kissinger believed that second strike capability had to become at least partially a preemptive strike or first strike capability. In Kissinger's proposal the existing ceiling for strategic weapons would therefore disappear. By choosing military objects as points of possible attack, the arms race could naturally continue.

What did the Chiefs of Staff do? I quote:

The joint Chiefs of Staff cooperated because they understood that the doctrine of assured destruction would inevitably lead to political decisions halting or neglecting the improvement of our strategic forces, and in time reducing them. We therefore developed in 1969 new criteria of strategic sufficiency, that related our strategic planning to the destruction of military targets as well.[10]

You have to rub your eyes to believe it. The arms race continued

because otherwise the "improvement" of American strategic
forces "threatened" to stop.

Here we hear from the mouth of an impeccable witness what
happens when a nation deems the goal of guaranteed security to
be of paramount importance. It develops the most modern technological means possible and gives that development free rein in
its economic system. At a certain moment those means begin to
govern themselves. For their "improvement" *they* demand new
possibilities of use; *they* coerce their users to develop new strategies which will again give them room to maneuver. The means
take control. The strategy no longer holds the weapons in check.
Instead, the progress of weapons technology determines the
strategy.

Later Developments
From that moment on the arms race raced ahead furiously. The
possibility of beginning and even waging a "limited nuclear war"
on European soil with strategic nuclear weapons worked its way
into NATO planning, a limited war which according to the conservative estimates of Carl Friedrich von Weiszacker would leave
ten million dead. In 1979 the European NATO partners wel-
comed the proposal to install strategic, military targeted, middle-
range nuclear missiles on European soil. They preferred that to
increasing their own conventional weapons. The aims of the
United States and their European allies, however, conflicted on
this point. The United States sought the "modernization" of
European military forces, so as not to be faced with the need to
use their own strategic nuclear forces in a conflict, at the penalty
of suicide. They advocated "decoupling." The European countries, however, favored deployment of the American missiles because they desired "linkage" with American strategic nuclear
forces and the mobilization of those forces when necessary.

NATO members played a poker game on a global table, and the lives of millions were the stakes.

Between 1970 and 1980 weapons trade across the world more than doubled.[11] Like cancer spreading through the body, the capacity to build nuclear bombs spread to many countries. In the image of an old story, the genie came out of Aladdin's lamp and could not be put in again. The world began to live in fear over what could come of this staggering proliferation of means of destruction. Meanwhile, negotiations over "arms control" (a phrase which Alva Myrdal has said should never have been coined) continued, leading to the result that under SALT I America and Russia gave each other permission to build two nuclear bombs a day. Under the SALT II accords that number was expanded to three and a half bombs a day. This was SALT II, where people said that America went too far! Weapons control became a camouflage allowing both sides to maintain a relentless arms race, a race extending even into outer space.

Recent events at the disarmament negotiations in Geneva only reinforce this picture. The centerpiece of these talks has been President Reagan's "zero option," under which NATO would have forgone deploying 108 Pershing II ballistic missiles and 464 Tomahawk cruise missiles in Europe if the Soviet Union had dismantled its entire arsenal of SS-20 missiles. Two comments must be made about this offer. First, the initiative had a one-sidedness which was obvious at first glance. The exchange proposed was that one side would not deploy under the condition that the other side would dismantle. For this reason NATO could not expect—and probably did not expect—the Soviet Union to take it seriously. Second, the proposal was extremely limited. It addressed only one type of weapon. In no way did it stop President Reagan from increasing pressure on Congress to approve his new MX missile system. Nor did it hinder him in the least from delivering his famous "star wars" speech on March 23, 1983, in which he called on the scientific community "to mobilize its efforts and resources in quest of an impenetrable antiballistic missile shield over the entire nation—without triggering perilously destabilizing countermeasures, both offensive and defensive, on the part of the USSR."[12]

What could have come from the Geneva negotiations under these circumstances? The most we could have expected was President Reagan's "interim" solution, which because of pressure on all fronts followed his initial one-sided offer. Under it at least a substantial number of Pershing II and/or Tomahawk missiles will be placed on European soil, regardless of other developments. The precise number will depend on the Soviet Union's readiness to negotiate. In other words: irrespective of whether or not Geneva "succeeds," an increase in nuclear weapons by the West is certain. Unfortunately, Geneva has served as little more than a fig leaf hiding the shame of a rapidly increasing arms race and deceiving a well-intentioned public on both sides.

A Complete Ideology

The history of the weapons question makes the presence of a complete security ideology unmistakable. All the trademarks of an ideology are present.

To begin with, many nations and groups of people today are possessed by the goal of guaranteed security. Their obsession gives them the impulse to use every means at their disposal and to create new strategies for reaching their all-encompassing end.

Also present are the *means:* weapons of massive destruction. The end justifies threatening others with their possible use. Weapons development is judged by no other standard than maximum precision and destructive power, to the point of absurdity. We do this in spite of the early warning of Eisenhower:

It happens that defense is a field in which I have had varied experience over a lifetime, and if I have learned anything, it is that there is no way in which a country can satisfy the craving for absolute security—but it easily can bankrupt itself, morally and economically, in attempting to reach that illusory goal through arms alone.[13]

Third, norms are distorted. Commonly known mandates of international law, which are inscribed in authorized treaties, do not interfere in the least with the further development of weapons technology, or even with the recently renewed production of chemical weapons. The law of self-protection at any price has replaced international law. Reports of political parties sometimes publicly and unashamedly advocate a double morality. They admit that the use or threat of use of nuclear weapons is morally and ethically objectionable, and even absolutely forbidden. But they argue that in the political reality of today, such weapons are indispensable.[14] "Goal morality" wins out. We adjust morality and ethics to the pursuit of national security.

The command to love is also ideologically distorted. Loving our neighbor is seen as protecting fellow human beings and fellow Christians in the West, but never or scarcely as protecting fellow humans behind the Iron Curtain. Solidarity is narrowed to solidarity with our allies alone.

The security ideology also forms an image of the enemy. The Leninist motive of world domination is easily attributed to every move that the Soviet Union makes, including its peace proposals. In marvelous contrast the China image is retouched; weapons may now be exported to China, even though Chinese communism is one of the most aggressive forms of contemporary communism.

But the ideological image of the enemy is most obvious when "the struggle against communism" becomes the constant motivation for strengthening Western armaments. The question may then be asked: how do people conceive of communism today? Is it a spiritual movement and a dangerous ideology, or is it something which can be defeated *militarily*? A little reflection shows that ideologies can be fought only with spiritual weapons. A military attack calls for a military defense, but an advancing ideology requires a spiritual defense. It is therefore a mistake, and a fruit of ideological thinking, to exacerbate existing military tensions in the world for the sake of fighting communism (or capitalism). Then deploying every military means is fully legitimated by the desire to battle a *demon,* such as the demonic communist ideology. Are not all means legitimate when resisting the devil? We no longer think in terms of the possible mass destruction of Russian *citizens*—including innocent women and children. Instead we think only in terms of smashing an intolerable demon. Against that demon we permit ourselves the most hideous means of destruction. But have we not then fallen prey to an ideology equally as totalitarian as communism?

The final step of idol worship—the role reversal of idol and idol worshiper—is also present. This reversal indicates that the range of the ideology is absolute. Though initially we thought ourselves able to use and control weapons technology, the reality is that increasingly it controls us. We surrender to the further testing and expansion of the arsenal of destruction, an arsenal which years ago went over our heads. A god has arisen, and fear and hypnosis are its tools of terror. We trust it for our security. It requires unbearable financial sacrifice and perhaps even human sacrifice, like the Old Testament Molech, for whom the people of Judah "burned their sons and daughters in the fire."[15] Why else does the systematic accumulation of means of mass destruction continue?

Annihilation belongs to the very nature of these demonic

means, even though our intention is never to use such weapons for the purpose of annihilation. The real question is therefore whether in critical situations we will still have the freedom to act in accordance with our intentions. A few years ago United States Secretary of Defense Donald Rumsfeld stated brazenly: "We do not exclude the possibility that for the defense of our interests we will be the first to use nuclear weapons."[16]

We must realize that gods never loosen their grip on people. If nations choose gods, they become slaves to their gods. Gandhi once said that the personality of a man changes when he acquires a weapon, and Churchill observed that if the military could run its course, it would fortify the moon. At some point those who want to protect life at any cost may feel that their weapons systems themselves leave them no choice but to use them. No doubt that feeling is a form of illusion, of hypnosis. Weapons systems do not live and cannot force us to use them. But in genuine idolatry they *do*. Consider the history of NATO strategy: we first considered the use of nuclear weapons *impossible* (1948), later *improbable* (1970), still later *probable* (with the rise of the concept of a limited nuclear war in 1979), and now some experts say that their use is *inevitable*. Only an ideology which has aroused a full-grown idolatry can accomplish this complete reversal.

Conclusion

In the previous chapters we have studied four ideologies in action. Ideologies are spiritual forces which direct and lead us, often at an unconscious level. We may now draw at least one conclusion.

No goal or end, however lofty or worthwhile, may allow us to elevate the means outside the reach of genuine truth, justice and the love of God and neighbor. This principle holds whether the goal is maintaining a Christian culture, eliminating the most malicious powers, protecting our deepest freedoms or even pursuing disarmament.[17] For as soon as the means become independent, they also become our gods, gods which will ultimately destroy us.

Our society has only two paths before it. The first is to commit our lives to biblical ways: to live justly, to love our neighbors and to manage God's creation as good stewards. This is the path of obedience, the way of God's law, the Torah.[18] It does not mean that we renounce all personal and societal goals. But as soon as our goals do not square with these deepest life principles, then we *must* either let our goals fall by the wayside or else drastically readjust them.

The second path is to commit our lives to our own goals. Such a course will redefine the biblical standards and rules for life. It will determine what freedom and justice are, and even how we read the Bible.[19] The means which we need to accomplish our purposes will then torment us unceasingly. We will nevertheless embrace them, whether we admit it or not. We will convince ourselves that we have no other choice, or that no one in life ever escapes getting his or her hands dirty. We will justify our behavior because our overarching goal hangs in the balance.

No other paths exist, either personally or politically. Either we give biblical norms priority and relativize our goals or we give our goals priority and relativize biblical norms.

A great tension exists therefore in our day between the gospel and ideology, between following Jesus and serving idols. The contrast is razor-sharp. There was only one way that Christ could conquer the powers of this world and make a public spectacle of them: He did not seek his own well-being, he distanced himself from every pursuit of power, and he preferred to obey God's commands rather than to look after his own identity as the Son of God.[20]

It seems that many Christians have systematically suppressed this knowledge of their Savior. They have selected their own goals, delivered themselves over to various ideologies, and thus have unwittingly worshiped demonic powers. They have built their own empire rather than God's kingdom. Following that course has been the deepest cause of their political fragmentation. It has been the *ruin* of the Christian church.

CHAPTER 7

The
Monstrous
Alliance

THE IDEOLOGIES OF REVOLUTION, NATION, MATERIAL PROSPER-
ity and guaranteed security differ in many ways. They differ not
only in the degree to which they are active but also in their means.
The revolution ideology uses armed resistance, while the prosperity ideology requires peaceful economic and technological
growth. The prosperity ideology regards the state as the welfare
state. The nationalist ideology sees it as an internal police state.
And the security ideology views it primarily as part of an international military alliance.

Often these ideologies stand in direct conflict with each other.
For example, the nationalist and revolution ideologies conflict in
South Africa and South America. A bitter ideological struggle re-
sults. Nations and power blocs may directly oppose each other

when, pursuing both the nationalist and security ideologies, they attempt to defend their identity with every means at their disposal. The tense relation between the "free West" and the "communist bloc" is laden with a series of ideological contradictions. Friction also exists between similar ideologies: the Western prosperity ideology collides with the Russian drive for economic expansion, and Western and Russian security objectives continually clash.

Because of their many differences in nature and elaboration, the dominant ideologies divide the world into many camps. These ideologies seem to be aimed at each other. The free West opposes the communist bloc, the governments of South Africa and South America trample guerrilla movements, and the Islamic oil countries resist "Zionist" Israel. The divisions among Christians mirror these global divisions. Christians embrace or reject the class struggle, defend or renounce nuclear weapons and support or oppose strong government, abortion, nuclear energy and liberation movements. Though often they express reservations about the most extreme consequences of their ideologies, Christians nevertheless give them their willing and active support.

Ideological Teamwork
In this chapter the conflicts between ideologies will not be foremost. What is more important and less clear is that, in spite of or even because of their oppositions, ideologies also play into each other's hands.

That ideologies cooperate in spite of their oppositions is not so difficult to see. The Western world, for example, tends to commit itself to the prosperity, nationalist and security ideologies, while the communist world links the prosperity and security ideologies to its own revolution ideology. South African and South American regimes govern by means of a combination of the nationalist and prosperity ideologies. Arab countries (such as

Iran and Libya) pursue these ideologies in their own way and attach them to certain forms of the revolution ideology. Clearly then certain combinations of ideologies are possible. Sometimes a country or power bloc will link various ideologies together into one whole, though not without problems. In South Africa the growth in prosperity threatens the policy of "separate development," and in the West every increase in defense spending threatens the standard of living. China and Russia vacillate between giving priority to world revolution, to expanding their militaries and to improving internal prosperity. Regularly they shift the accent. Yet many ties link these and other opposing ideologies together, ties strengthened by technological, economic and scientific forces of modernization. Though ideologies may battle each other with fire and sword, they also cross-fertilize and cooperate. Business, for example, has an economic interest in expanding weapons exports, and the military has an interest in strengthening economic growth.

But that ideologies work together by means of their contradictions seems to be a crass form of logic. Nevertheless it is true. One ideology can call another into being through a sort of diabolical or dialectical play. Or, as if in a relay race, one ideology can pass the baton on to another, even within the same time period. It can do this by means of existing contradictions. This form of ideological teamwork deserves our closer attention.

Ideologies in History. A quick sketch of twenty centuries of world history will support the thesis that conflicting ideologies often call each other into being.

Christianity arose within the strong but oppressive Roman Empire. Though initially the church was entirely separate from the empire, in the fourth century Constantine forged a link between the state and the church. Christianity then became the official religion of the state. At the end of his life Constantine was baptized in white clothes: throne and altar came together.

The Constantinian period lasted for many centuries. The Roman Empire became the Holy Roman Empire, which forced the gospel on unwilling people with its bow and stamped out all pagan opposition under its crown. As a joint and established power, the church and state formulated laws and demanded the love of all its subjects. The church punished civil crimes by means of sacramental exclusion and excommunication. An inflexible nationalist ideology had arisen, because the goal of protecting and expanding earthly power became all-important.

In the course of the centuries the fusion between church and state evoked opposition. The Renaissance and Reformation broke with the ecclesiastical exercise of political power. In some cases that break was made on the political terrain. England, along with The Netherlands and the Scandinavian countries, struggled free from the political dominion of the church. Large sections of Europe, however, still remained under the combined power of the church and state. In eighteenth-century France that power reached an absolute low point of tyranny and oppression, which paved the way for a new ideology: the ideology of revolution.

The French Revolution was a revolution soaked in blood. As the revolution killed its own children, the shedding of blood became a cult. We hear a later echo of the same revolution and struggle in Russia in 1917, where the revolutionaries struck against the allied power of the czarist throne and the Russian Orthodox altar. There too the cult of blood reigned. Lenin prepared the Russian people to wade through streams of blood.

The French Revolution altered the face of the Western world. New social relationships arose. The major conflict in society was no longer between peasant and noble or between peasant and clergy. Now, in the midst of great poverty, the class struggle became the predominant conflict, especially in Europe. Another all-encompassing goal then presented itself: overcoming poverty with every economic and technological means available.

As the industrial apparatus grew, a faith in inevitable progress and economic improvement spread throughout the entire population. Soon the state involved itself increasingly in the economic progress of society. With its newly formed socioeconomic criteria of justice, it determined which sectors of the population needed monetary assistance. Putting its socioeconomic planning into practice, the government entangled itself more and more in the division of the growing wealth. The ideology of material prosperity became firmly established.

As material prosperity climbed and the power of the state increased, more means to growth were necessary and more had to be protected. Soon a race began for the resource-rich areas of Africa, South America and Asia which were not yet under Western domination. New economic and political power blocs were built. Two world wars succeeded each other, the first motivated by the struggle over the colonies, the second by the economic and political expansion drives of colonyless Germany.

The repercussions of the two world wars have been enormous. Today the cry sounds for producing unprecedented political, technological and military means to prevent a possible repeat of these wars. If technology and the economy have brought us prosperity, then why can they not bring us security? A new security ideology has arisen in the wake of the prosperity ideology. It is an ideology more pale and relentless than those preceding it. Guaranteed security requires new forms of technological development. At the same time, however, anxiety rises as the mass production of these new technological means increases. For they are means which ultimately sow the seeds of death.

An Apocalyptic Vision. As if they were the principal actors in an apocalyptic vision, the four major ideologies prepared the way for each other. Each ushered in the next. The nationalist ideology summoned the revolution ideology, and the prosperity ideology aroused the security ideology. It is as if we perceive something of the voice in the book of Revelation summoning the four horses to begin their terrible journey over the earth:

> I watched as the Lamb opened the first of the seven seals. Then I heard one of the four living creatures say in a voice like thunder, "Come!" I looked, and there before me was a white horse! Its rider held a bow, and he was given a crown, and he rode out as a conqueror bent on a conquest.

> When the Lamb opened the second seal, I heard the second living creature say, "Come!" Then another horse came out, a fiery red one. Its rider was given power to take peace from the earth and to make men slay each other. To him was given a large sword.

> When the Lamb opened the third seal, I heard the third living creature say, "Come!" I looked, and there before me was a black horse! Its rider was holding a pair of scales in his hand. Then I heard what sounded like a voice among the four living creatures, saying, "A quart of wheat for a day's wages, and three quarts of barley for a day's wages, and do not damage the oil and the wine!"

> When the Lamb opened the fourth seal, I heard the voice of the fourth living creature say, "Come!" I looked, and there before me was a pale horse! Its rider was named Death, and Hades was following close behind him. They [the four horses] were given power over a fourth of the earth to kill by sword, famine and plague, and by the wild beasts of the earth.[1]

The Arms Spiral

Ideologies call each other into being. In spite of and because of their oppositions they form one family, which with masterful teamwork enslaves and oppresses the people of the world.

But their cooperation goes even further. Together they create today's *spirals,* which like violent whirlpools pull the world down and under. Through these spirals the cooperating powers are able to grip us and drag us along against our will. The spirals also give root to much of the fatalism of our day.

The arms spiral is the most obvious. Each rotation carries us further and further. Different ideologies set this spiral in motion. The security and revolution ideologies of both the East and West are certainly at work here. Yet the interaction of these ideologies does not explain the unbelievable, irreversible *momentum* of the arms race. For otherwise why would the East and West not be inclined to agree on a maximum number of weapons and a genuine balance of power? Surely an accord such as this would serve the security of both and would be consistent with Russia's reformulated ideology of revolution.

To finish the puzzle we need the piece of a third, equally active ideology: the prosperity ideology. It is this partner in the monstrous alliance which creates the irreversibility of the arms spiral.

The prosperity ideology has generated a vast production system and a continually self-renewing technology in the East and in the West. This production system and technology constantly explore new possibilities for expansion. As the means to material prosperity, however, they have become powers in themselves. They seize every opportunity to press forward, including moving into weapons production, weapons exports and weapons research.

In recent years this continual pressure for economic expansion has made the arms sector a "normal" and essential element of the whole production system in both the East and the West.

Thirty years ago one would still distinguish a separate weapons industry in every national economy, an industry more or less independent of the peacetime industry. It was a sort of vertical segment of the economy. But in today's modern economies nearly every industrial giant or multinational corporation plays a direct or indirect role in weapons production. This is true in the electronics industry (General Electric makes parts for the Trident submarine and the Mark 12A missile), the manufacturing industry (Rockwell International produces the neutron bomb, the navigational system of the Trident submarine and is involved in MX missile production), the office supply industry (Litton Industries makes cruise missile guidance systems), the commercial aircraft industry (Boeing produces the air-launched cruise missile), the automotive industry (Chrysler makes the M60 and Abrams M1 tanks) and the petrochemical industry (Monsanto, whose slogan is "without chemicals, life itself would be impossible," makes the explosive detonator of the hydrogen bomb). These are only a few examples. But they show that a growing number of people depend directly on weapons production for their employment. A recent United Nations report states: "In the United States in the late 1970s, 8 to 10 per cent of the labor force in manufacturing was engaged in the production of weapons and military equipment, or 1.5 to 1.8 million workers."[2] Is it any wonder then that our society exerts enormous economic pressure to maintain current weapons production for the sake of preserving income and work? And is it any surprise that the products are offered to friend and enemy alike?

Arming the enemy is perhaps the most explicit example of how opposing ideologies cooperate and reinforce each other. Not long ago it was established that Soviet missiles have highly valuable American parts in them. Recent reports speak of exports of enriched uranium from the Soviet Union to America. British

forces were attacked with British and French parts in the Falk-
lands war. And China has become an attractive market for American weapons exports.

So economic and technical pressure pulls the noose around the
world tighter, and the arms spiral is the inevitable result. Under
these circumstances weapons control becomes a facade or a
Band-Aid for a huge gash. Therefore, Alva Myrdal concluded
after her years of experience as a peace negotiator that East and
West are both strong in the *rhetoric* of arms control and disarmament, but "beneath the surface they have increasingly acted as if
there were between them a conspiracy not to permit a halt; still
less a reversal of the arms race."[3] When countries or power
blocs fall prey to an ideology, gradually they become victims of
the spirits and powers which they have evoked.

The Economic Spiral

The arms spiral is not the only spiral threatening today's world.
Another spiral has formed on the economic and monetary field.
Though less known, it is no less dangerous.

We begin again with the years 1969-70. Remember that in
1969 the United States recommitted itself to a strategic arms race,
breaking through its own ceiling of military sufficiency. But the
beginning of the seventies is of particular economic interest.
Then another ceiling was broken: the volume of money created
in the world. The United States severed the official tie between
gold and the dollar, thereby giving itself and other countries a
free hand to make dollars and other key currencies in enormous
quantities. According to the calculations of Robert Triffin, a
renowned monetary expert, the quantity of international currencies (dollars, yens, marks, francs and so on) available in the
world grew more in a three-year period (1969 to 1972) than in the
whole history of the world from Adam and Eve to 1969.[4]

What explains such a staggering explosion of money in the world? To make a long story short: every dollar made in the United States costs no more than its production costs. In the international exchange, however, it receives the full value of the dollar. When the United States created large quantities of dollars, the outgoing stream of dollars became a powerful mechanism allowing its economy to invest in other countries, to buy foreign companies and to channel military expenditures to foreign countries when necessary (as in Vietnam) at minimal expense. Prior to 1970 the tie to gold held the volume of money in check. But severing the tie—a strategy of the powerful expansion interests of the Western world—eliminated the restriction on international money creation. Money supply is an instrument necessary to the ideology of prosperity. It is a means whose necessity is dictated to us by our goal of material prosperity.

This fundamental step had consequences. When the flood of money poured over the world, naturally the value of the dollar and its related currencies dwindled. One could buy less with a dollar than before. Third World countries in particular were affected by this larceny—they received progressively less valuable dollars for the resources which they exported to the West. To the Third World countries which could still muster their strength, this was the signal to react strongly. A few formed the OPEC bloc, and its participating countries raised their oil prices. The first energy crisis was real. It was provoked by the Western countries themselves, which in their greed had no patience for limiting money supply and energy consumption. Today oil or energy is the Achilles heel of the large economies. Western nations had to pay billions of dollars more for their oil, and their balance of payments (that is, the relation between receivables and foreign debts) was lost. How did they respond to this imbalance? Did they restrict their investments, import less and take a step backward in their own prosperity? If you think so, then you underestimate the strength of the prosperity ideology, an ideology which requires maintaining the existing level of prosperity no matter what the cost. Struggling to maintain that level, the Western countries reacted in three ways.

First, they made new money! The money explosion increased instead of decreased. In the next three years, from 1972 to 1975, world money reserves doubled.[5] Second, they borrowed from the oil countries, which had become instantly rich. Enormous international credit was exchanged between states, making the burden of debt of many countries skyrocket. Third, they increased exports. These exports came mainly from the most technologically advanced sector of the Western economies: weapons production. In one year, from 1973 to 1974, the weapons exports of the United States doubled from four billion to eight billion dollars, due to the application of Nixon's new "arm our allies" doctrine.

What was the combined effect of these reactions? Making new money meant a new depreciation of the dollar. The price of the dollar tumbled. This drop meant again a lower return on exports to the oil countries. The expansion of weapons exports meanwhile raised the weapons ceiling in the world as a whole. The Arab countries saw the military arsenal of Israel grow, and at the same time they received less and less for their oil. Can you picture their reaction? They felt they had no choice but to raise their oil prices again.

That increase occurred in 1978, and the second energy crisis became a reality. The new crisis affected the Western balance of payments more seriously than the first, for from 1978 on the repeated shock therapy essentially decelerated Western economic growth. Both the Western countries' burden of debt and budget deficits reached hitherto unknown heights. Today we experience a stagnation of growth, a growing burden of debt and enormous financial deficits. Under such conditions interest rates rise and the weight of existing debts grows even heavier. The world economy today shakes at its foundation. There seems to be no cure for the economic problems that now ravage the world.

The poor developing countries are hit the hardest by the economic spiral. Unlike the oil countries, they cannot fight back or create new money to pay for what they want to buy. Those are the privileges of only the wealthy countries. The poorest countries therefore had to take the full blow of the higher energy prices, a blow which had much greater force than all the development aid granted to them since World War 2. And today they suffer the full consequences of higher interest rates and the current world recession. Meeting in Buenos Aires in March 1983, the "Group of 77" developing countries established that between 1980 and early 1983 at least 200 billion dollars were drained from the developing countries by higher interest rates, lower prices for raw materials and the protectionism of the industrial nations. Under these conditions the poor countries have no choice but to fall more deeply in debt. They must acquire new loans to pay the interest and principal on their existing loans—if, of course, international banks cooperate. But the burden of debt of the poor countries is already terribly high, and they threaten to collapse. Recently a commission of the International Monetary Fund ascertained that a large number of the poor countries can no longer fulfill their financial obligations and warned that we have now approached the time of the bankruptcy of national states. Between 1980 and 1982 the foreign debt of Brazil doubled, and currently Zambia, Bolivia, Argentina, Brazil, Mexico and Venezuela must pay more money on the interest and principal of their foreign debts than the total income they receive from exports.[6] Depending on fluctuations in the price of oil, national bankruptcy threatens both the oil-exporting developing countries, such as Mexico and Venezuela, and the oil-importing developing countries, such as Brazil, Argentina, Chile and Bangladesh.

How long can the world monetary system survive these absurd strains? Recently a number of banks have refused loans to the Third World, and those which grant new loans fear the possible consequence: default on loans still outstanding. Will the expected recovery of economic growth in the world alleviate this situation? Very likely it will not. For only fantastic growth in the Third World *itself* would allow the developing countries to meet their financial obligations. And such growth is precisely what the wealthy Western countries cannot and will not tolerate. The pursuits of their own material prosperity and of the protection of their borders do not permit it.

The collapse of the entire monetary system is therefore the most likely prospect. In the last article before her death Barbara Ward predicted that, barring a change in the West, we face the collapse of the existing world monetary system and a world crisis which will not even compare with the bleakness of the thirties.[7]

The End of the Spirals

Am I a prophet of doom? No, I am not. We must approach today's problems more seriously than that. Never have I spoken of an external fate which controls us. These whirlpools are our own doing, for only the mixture of our ideologies can create spirals.

But, you may ask, why do the whirlpools continue even if people begin to reflect on and even reject their ideologies? This is an important question, because today's whirlpools are drawing us to a frightening destination. The arms spiral will not end, it seems, until either the earth's vital resources give out or until the world itself is destroyed by its weapons. The economic spiral pulls us down toward a world economic crisis, a crisis from which the wealthy Western countries may recover but which will ruin the poorest countries of the world. It seems that our spirals will cease only in chaos, annihilation, the exhaustion of the world's resources and the ruin of the poor. Why then do we let these spirals go on? Is our crisis a question of a lack of insight, or of a lack of the will?

My answer goes deeper than pinning the blame on the power of inherently evil societal structures or technology. The truth is that we have allowed ourselves to be seduced and hypnotized. Ideology, we saw earlier, is the conduit of idolatry. And with idolatry the elements of seduction and hypnosis come into play. Idols cast a hypnotic spell on us.

Only the demonic can cast such a powerful spell. If we look closely, we perceive something of the activity of the great opponent of God. He alone can seduce persons and nations, possess them, and pull them down into the Abyss of chaos, disintegration and destruction. He can do this only if time and again we allow ourselves to be lured by our ideologies. It is as if today the kingdom of darkness plays a brutal game of enticement on a global scale, alternately using the seductions of the revolution, nation, prosperity and security ideologies to divide people and to draw all of them into an Abyss from which there is no escape. Divide and conquer—that is the strategy of the kingdom of the Abyss.

CHAPTER 8

Hope
Awakens
Life

THE SUBJECT MATTER OF THIS BOOK IS HARDLY UPLIFTING. WE have traced vigorous ideologies to which nations and peoples cling. We have discussed the rise of autonomous powers which impose their will on us as gods. And we have spoken of ominous spirals, which like whirlpools pull us down and under. These spirals seem to cast a demonic spell on us, a spell which allows the demonic to "divide and conquer." At first glance I might be accused of the most depressing variation of fatalistic thinking that one can imagine.

To make matters worse, I have pictured ideologies as spiritual movements which drive their adherents to grisly extremes. The communist ideology, for example, lends the Soviet Union a mood of aggression which it tries to vent with equal force on the Polish

people and the Third World. The possibility of Soviet aggression
reinforces Western ideologies of security and enhances the at-
traction of protecting national identity and material prosperity
at any price. This reaction then provokes further Russian aggression. There seems to be no way out of this ideological cycle. For
has not a world view of fear and anxiety arisen which merely
drives people and nations even more forcefully into the arms of
their economic, technological and scientific idols?

Fatalism
Yet in no way do the ominous signs of our situation necessitate
fatalism or doomsday thinking. Doomsday thinking portrays the
future as an inevitable *fate* which will fall over us unexpectedly
and against our will. Nothing will overcome this fate—neither
fighting, nor praying nor fleeing. Doomsday thinking offers no
spark of hope; instead, it drowns out all hope. As such it is one
of the most dangerous deceptions of our time.

Where did today's fatalism come from? Did it arise from a
realistic assessment of the seriousness of contemporary problems? If so, then we should embrace it as an attitude toward life
with more integrity than the artificial optimism practiced by
many today. However, the roots of doomsday thinking are more
sinister.

Let me explain. Given the opportunity, idols govern not only
the behavior but also the spirits of men and women. They hypno-
tize the human spirit, captivating it by their seemingly overwhelming power. Every form of genuine idol worship in the
world, even among so-called primitive people, includes hypnosis.
Consciousness alters. People see the present and future only
within the limited perspective of the environment which sur-
rounds them and their idol. The reality outside of their situation
either fades away altogether or is seen only within a parochial

perspective. This narrowing of focus and awareness then nurtures the breathtaking suggestion that *the gods* hold our fate in their hands. They decree and we listen, even if they lead us to our doom.

This narrowing of focus is the origin of doomsday thinking. Doomsday thinking is nothing less than the final and definitive prostration before the idols of the day. It agrees that the gods control our fate. In its own way it adapts fully to their lordship; it accepts and works within the narrow limitations established by the idols.

The great error of Western society during the Enlightenment was its belief that it could eliminate every form of magic, superstition and religious fear once and for all. Enlightenment society believed that reason, or levelheaded and rational deliberation, would drive away the shadows of the past. Even today some scientists can become outraged if one suggests that the power of their own products has mesmerized and hypnotized them, making them slaves of one or another form of idolatry. Certainly, they say, our scientific activity is as objective and rational as possible! But rationality alone is no antidote to idolatry. Sometimes it even contributes to idolatry. Rationality can easily become a tool allowing people to think in narrower and narrower circles. Such a closed yet relentless train of thought mirrors the scientists who equate the world with the data which their limited systems observe and apprehend.

Ours is a day of imprisoned expertise. The expertise of economists is imprisoned in their systems which presuppose the infinity of human desires and needs—needs which they, servants of the insatiability of Western men and women, will help to satisfy. The expertise of technicians is imprisoned in the principle that what technology *can* do it *must* do, while the decision of what to do with its products belongs to others. The expertise of military experts is imprisoned in the pursuit of absolute military security and certainty. In spite of or even because of their rationality most scientists and experts today are the *ministers* of the dominant ideologies. Again and again their oracles serve the goals of maximum security or maximum prosperity, and again and again they enslave us to the ruthless means to these ends.

Where then is the hope? Where is the alternative to fatalism and the strength to break out of the magic circles and whirlpools of our day?

Circle and Cross.   In his famous book *Orthodoxy*[1] G. K. Chesterton states that most modern thinkers strike him as lunatic, as people who have lost all sense. He too finds the same combination of logical completeness and spiritual poverty, the same strict logical compression of reality into extremely narrow circles. Chesterton may carry this too far. But his contribution is most significant when he juxtaposes the image of the closed circle with the openness of the cross:

> The circle is perfect and infinite in its nature; but it is fixed forever in its size; it can never be larger or smaller. But the cross, though it has at its heart a collision and a contradiction, can extend its four arms forever without altering its shape. Because it has a paradox in its centre it can grow without changing. The circle returns upon itself and is bound. The cross opens its arms to the four winds; it is a support for free travellers.[2]

Symbols have a relative value. But their truth sometimes reaches deep. There is truth in this image for us, who in our personal and societal worlds are imprisoned in cramped circles and pinched spirals: the only escape possible is *in and through the cross* of our suffering and prevailing Messiah. All efforts to survive and maintain life *at any cost* must be crucified, following Christ's own example. We must reject any means or ends which replace obedience to the will and law of God. This is the collision and contradiction which Chesterton pointed to. They take place within our *hearts*. The cross of Jesus Christ therefore has a significance reaching much deeper than our personal salvation. The apostle Paul describes the cross as a victory over the powers of this world: "On that cross he discarded the cosmic powers and authorities like a garment; he made a public spectacle of them and led them as captives in his triumphal procession."[3]

What powers did Christ conquer? The answer lies in the nature of Christ's suffering. Jesus died in complete poverty, in the renouncing of all earthly power and in the abandonment of his divine identity. In dying this death he became stronger than the powers of the kingdom of the abyss, which seduce and imprison people and nations in their relentless search for wealth, power and a sure identity. Despite their assault on the cross, these powers were impotent against Jesus. Defenseless and on display, the Messiah defeated them and triumphed over them publicly. The cross of Christ delivered the mortal blow to all the powers of the abyss, whether they are called Mammon, Molech, or Baal,[4] or whether in our day they are clothed in the disguise of the revolution, nationalist, prosperity and security ideologies.

No other power will eliminate the circles and snares of the dominant ideologies. No other power will expose the hypnosis which ideologies spread. Divided Christianity and the fear-filled world must accept the Crucified One by crucifying their obsessions with ends! Only then will resurrection and liberation take place.

The way of resurrection does exist. The cross stood in *this* world. Though this world seems consigned to death, the resurrected Messiah is still its only lawful heir. The creation will be given to him, not to demons. He still sustains this world by the word of his power, and after every thunderstorm a rainbow still shines as a sign of God's readiness to preserve, not destroy.

Many Christians today still believe in the dualistic god of Greco-Roman religion, the Janus-faced god who as Almighty Power or Providence created evil as well as good, and who arbitrarily either loves us or hurls us to destruction. That god is not the God of Scripture. Yahweh is true to his Word. He remains faithful to what he has promised and loves his Word as his own Son. We may continually remind him of his promises; we may hold him to them.

The deadly danger of this dualistic theology is that it attributes the work of the demonic kingdom to God himself. Therefore it cannot discern the strategies of the demonic kingdom for ensnaring nations and peoples. As a result it makes the enduring promises of the God of Israel powerless, just as in a different way liberal theology has tried to silence the living God, maintaining that his saving acts, both past and present, never happened and never will.

The Morning Star
Probably because of these theologies many Christians have lost hope and simply do not understand the essence of Christian hope. For many of us, hope comes only by the grace of a few tiny cracks in the wall which throw slivers of light on our bleak situation. That hope is then extinguished as one by one the cracks disappear and the darkness envelops us. But this is the opposite of Christian hope! Christian hope is a hope of contrast: it revives in the *middle of the night,* just when the darkness seems to overpower us.

The biblical image of hope is the morning star. The morning star often appears between two and three at night, when the darkness is complete and the faintest sign of morning is not yet visible. So small that it threatens to vanish, the star seems unable to vanquish the overpowering darkness. Yet when you see the morning star, you know that the night has been defeated. For the morning star pulls the morning in behind it, just as certainly as Jesus pulls the kingdom in behind him. "I am the morning star." These were Jesus' last words to us. They appear on the last page of every Bible.

How do we act on this image of hope? The example of Esther can help us here. F. Weinreb, a vilified Jewish scholar, has written an impressive book on the story of Esther under the title *I Who Am Hidden*.[5] The I who is hidden is the Lord of the Covenant. His name never appears in the book of Esther. Fate, not the Lord, seems to be center stage. The decision to eliminate the people of Israel was written in the unbreakable laws of the Medes and Persians and sealed by the emperor. The Lord seemed absent. But Esther's name means "morning star"! "Who knows," Esther's stepfather Mordecai said to her, "but that you have come to royal position for such a time as this?"[6] So late on Passover morning, after the Jewish feasts had finished, and trembling with fear, Esther went to the king, who raised his scepter to her.

Esther's simple walk to the king was the turning point in Israel's story of fate. Miracles did not save Israel, at least not miracles as we understand them. But as a Father who works hiddenly, God linked his saving acts to the act of Esther, who in obedience put her own life in jeopardy. *That* act God blessed. That was the act which he, the Doer, waited for in hiding. "When Esther appears," writes Weinreb, "when Esther is seen in the darkness of the exile, that is the sign of daybreak. Where God in his hiddenness can be delineated, there is the sign that the defeat of the night has come."[7]

Living out of messianic hope is therefore different from just waiting passively. It requires that we leave our protective shelters behind and put our future, our prosperity, and if necessary our whole life in jeopardy for the sake of truth and justice. We must do this not because we ourselves are somehow able to dismantle today's demonic spirals and deified powers. Rather, we must do it because the Torah tells us that our acts of undistorted justice and unperverted love in the midst of powerful ideologies can be a sign to the living God to unite his saving acts to ours. Our acts can be a call for the mobilization of the forces of God's kingdom in a time of doom, just as Esther's act was centuries ago. Who knows whether the God who is hidden waits for just that? We do not need to know precisely how to take the first risky step or what the exact outcome of the spiritual battle will be. "Who knows?"— Mordecai said that too. Like us, he did not have a corner on wisdom. But we *must* take that first step.

Christian hope connects rather than disconnects us from the contemporary situation. Though the appeal to abandon our idols and deceitful ideologies is addressed to all of us, the nature and difficulty of the first step will differ according to our situation. Breaking with a rigid nationalist ideology in our midst requires different first steps than abandoning the security or prosperity ideologies. But for all the variation of steps, the appeal remains the same. We must break publicly with those *means* in which we have put our faith, and we must distance ourselves from those *goals* which define the meaning of life for us. These goals and means form barriers to practical obedience and to genuine, non-ideological love. They restrain us from doing concrete works of justice to those who oppress us and from exercising truth and mercy wherever pressure or even blackmail is used against us. For one the cost of obeying the appeal will be his reputation, for another her political party or church, for a third his community, and for a fourth his or her life. But risking a first step is the only option for those who answer to the hope which lives within us.

The First Step

How can we take the first step? How can we motivate ourselves
and others to risk the hazards of such a step? We cannot simply
plead for a change in mentality. Pleas of this sort are too shallow
and have been used too often. People do not really change if their
hearts do not change, if they are not willing to reject their goals
and adjust their means. This spiritual struggle for the heart has
been the subject of this book. And I have addressed myself especially to Christians, not to provoke a little family squabble but to
level a deep criticism. How can we expect national conversion
if we Christians do not admit that we too are accomplices in the
basic wrongs of our country and of the world? We must be the first
to confess the guilt of pursuing ideologies and serving other gods.
We must also and especially give the preaching of the gospel the
deep dimension needed for our time. Then we may call the nation to repentance. That appeal is the real mission of the church
today, for it is not the liberation of the church but of the nations
and peoples of this world which is at stake.

In North America and Europe the nationalist, security and
prosperity ideologies are predominant. Day by day the spirals
which they set in motion divide us. What might be a first step
at dismantling these spirals?

I shall conclude this book by sketching the outlines of a possible
first step. I offer this sketch to you as part of the search for the
smooth stone we need to slay our Goliaths. I do not have a corner
on wisdom either. But we may be sure of one thing: it must be a
step by which we dare to stand within and against today's dynamic
whirlpools and spirals. Our step will therefore be characterized
by the word *enough,* not by the words *more and more.*

The Security Ideology Revisited.   The security ideology becomes
most inflexible in the realm of political debate. Different factions
argue over the best way to guarantee "our" security. One pleads

for limiting nuclear weapons, the other for increasing them. But both sides scoff at the question of whether the threat or use of such weapons is justifiable. Yet for Christians this question is the heart of the whole issue.

Do the newly developed weapons and technologies still fulfill the requirements of just use during periods of war? Do certain new weapons still fall within the yardstick of legitimacy? The Torah has the answer. The Old Testament laws forbid the use of gruesome methods of warfare against and even by *pagan* nations.[8] During war soldiers were to spare the lives of women, children and livestock.[9] Further, the laws forbid the people of Israel from using the most advanced weapon of the day—the chariot. Why then must the means and methods of warfare remain outside of the political discussion, even when those means blatantly violate all the written and unwritten rules of international law all across the centuries? And if Russia resorts to producing chemical weapons, is *that* sufficient grounds for NATO to add them to its own arsenal of destruction? We condemn totalitarian states and their totalitarian ends. But have not we ourselves embraced totalitarian means?

We must refuse every possible use of these means absolutely, no matter how risky such a refusal may be. We have a higher mandate to obey than that of Chernenko or Reagan. Every further step on our part in the arms race is evil, even if others provoke us to continue it. Caught in the tension created by the overpowering arms spiral, North America and Europe must in obedience *refuse* to store and produce more nuclear and chemical weapons, and they must refuse their possible first *and* second use. We have enough of these terrible weapons!

For its part, Europe must refuse not just the Pershing II and cruise missiles. It must also refuse the American guarantee to protect Europe by means of American strategic nuclear arms.

Europe has no right to accept these means of terror for its own protection. Europeans know first hand the devastation which these demonic weapons can inflict. They may not pursue their own protection at the price of the possible destruction of other nations, such as the United States. Europe must publicly reject nuclear assistance from its NATO allies, for such aid is a demonic form of help.

How will North America and Europe muster the courage to take this step of refusal, which begins with a nuclear freeze? Perhaps by reading the old laws and promises of God's covenant with new eyes, by rereading the prophecy of Isaiah,[10] and by listening again to the Psalms, which tell us that the chariots of God stand above us thousands of thousands strong—more protection than ten thousand megatons of destruction.[11] God's covenant does not demand that we reject all defense efforts. But Europe and the United States must reject means of destruction which violate the undistorted laws of justice and righteousness in the Torah. They must place their final security in the hands of God, who can and who will fulfill his promises to persons and nations.

There are not two sides to God's promises, an Old Testament side and a New Testament side. If Jews and Christians have grown apart over the centuries, it is because Jews have stressed the law, the Torah, and Christians have stressed the gospel. As long as that atrocious opposition between law and gospel or between the Torah and the good news exists, Jews and Christians will never cross the gulf separating them. In the global darkness of today, in which the spirals of evil churn on, a path may become visible on which Jews and Christians may walk together. For their part Christians must begin to take seriously the basic principles of justice, mercy and love in the Torah. They must see it as a law which in Christ gives life. They must hold firmly to the Torah in the midst of ridicule and pressure, for it holds open the promise of deliverance. Deliverance will come even if Christians must bear their cross and suffer, as many faithful Jews did during World War 2 and during their return to the country of Israel. At this deep level, the level of the Torah, Christians and Jews must again hold hands, returning to the common Source from which they came.

The Prosperity Ideology Revisited.   We have also put our faith in means other than modern weapons. We cling to rising economic growth and technological progress just as desperately as we do to arms. And now we face an economic dead end too.

Economic life today is like a fish swimming into a net. The fish wants to get out, but it sees no alternative other than swimming more and more frantically into the net. It squirms hopelessly, when meanwhile one abrupt movement backward would probably return it to the freedom for which it yearns.

Today we produce and produce in order to maintain and increase our incomes, protect our consumption abilities and preserve our material well-being. But we swim continually into our own self-made net. Why not take one abrupt and perhaps painful movement back from the economic goal which hypnotizes us? Why not accept a possibly painful drop in our levels of income and consumption and orient ourselves to a level of *enough,* so that our production process will meet the most elementary requirements of the Torah?

Let me explain. If we take the demands of stewardship seriously, then human dignity in work must be primary. Stewardship, a basic principle of the Torah, requires the use of technologies which are sufficiently labor intensive and which suit human beings and their realm of responsibility. It sets strict limitations on the plunder of the environment. If one honors these requirements (thus having enough flexibility to reject objectionable defense contracts or to abandon risky forms of energy develop-

ment), then income and consumption levels will indeed drop. On
the average these levels will be lower than the levels to which we
are now accustomed. But we will have deliberately chosen them
for the sake of meaningful work, a clean environment and a sufficient amount of extra income for transfer to the poorest countries. We will have moved from biblical norms to responsible production and consumption levels.

Our current economic thinking and social system work in the
opposite direction of the Torah. Maintaining economic growth is
our first priority. *Then* arise questions of what to do with the resulting unemployment, the dehumanization of work, the rape of
the environment and other problems. Our priorities constrain
us to use increasingly large-scale technologies and to accept weapons contracts from wherever they come. These are obvious signs
of our slavery to an ideology of prosperity.

No shalom awaits those who follow this ideology. If we seriously desire to leave it, we must learn to make substantial economic
reallocation toward a maintenance economy. And our businesses,
labor unions, political parties and other organizations—and we
ourselves—must urgently move in that direction.

As with the armaments issue, taking a first step in breaking
with the ideology of prosperity cannot happen without a willingness to sacrifice. A clenched fist solves nothing; giving back what
we have undeservedly received does. A refusal of arms and a reversal of economic priorities may seem like a suicidal leap from a
tall building, a leap into the darkness. But inside the building a
fire has begun, and we have the promise of a good safety net far
below. It is the net of God's undeserved blessing, the return of
his friendly face.

A Policy Proposal.   I shall try to make the steps regarding armaments and prosperity a little more concrete by combining them
within a specific policy proposal.

Today's stress on weapons puts heavy pressure on our economies. Official figures tell us that in Europe an average of 24.4% of central government expenditures, or nearly one-fourth, goes to arms. The corresponding figure in North America is 22.6%.[12] At the same time, government deficits have soared. Even fiscally conservative President Reagan was forced to propose the largest budget deficit in American history, because in spite of his high cuts in social services he did not want to decrease his defense program. But suppose for a moment that a number of countries curtailed their weapons efforts and cut back their weapons expenditures. In and of itself nothing positive would come of this change: unemployment would only increase. But suppose again that year by year the monies which this shift freed up were earmarked for two purposes. First, the monies would cancel the debts of the poorest countries of the world and relieve them of their interest payments—under the condition that these countries would also decrease their weapons expenditures. Second, the monies would be used to create additional employment in our own countries. This employment would be directed at areas and people that we have abandoned: the environment, people in mental-health institutions, the quality of human labor and the inhabitability of our rotting cities.

What could we expect from this move? A double measure of healing could come. First, the poorest developing countries would gradually be rid of their oppressive financial burdens and be able to grow peacefully. In *their* growth and in *their* well-being could lie *our* peace. Peaceful trade with them could flourish. Second, the United States and Europe would begin an economic *conversion,* fulfilling to some degree Isaiah's prophecy that nations "will beat their swords into plowshares and their spears into pruning hooks."[13] The biblical image of the pruning hook suggests doing something with labor-intensive care. Conversion is possible if we do not make selfish income demands and if we pattern ourselves after an economy of care, an economy of enough.

Today very few people would want to work in an economy of care. We have indeed "tilled the earth," but we have systematically avoided the second half of our mandate, namely, "to take care of it."[14] Therein lie the labor possibilities of the future. The loss caused by decreasing our weapons expenditures would return to us by way of the poorest countries and by way of conversion in our own country. If we lessen our financial demands, government deficits will decrease too. Our spirals will then start to spin in the other direction, especially in the poorest countries. If we realign our economies, then the poor countries can pursue the peaceful reconstruction of their economies. But such reconstruction will take place only if the poor countries cooperate and only if we give them the opportunity.

The words of Isaiah challenge us with a threefold appeal today. They urge us to reduce defense spending, to channel the unclaimed monies to the poorest countries, and to build an economy of care, an economy of *enough*. Will our governments, labor unions, businesses, other organizations and we ourselves listen to the appeal? The words of Isaiah were not just intended as prophecy; they were also intended as a personal and national economic program.

It is time to put that program in place—not because the program itself can help us, but because its implementation will be a sign of our willingness to repent, to turn our ways to the only One who can and will help us. Perhaps this is the act of Esther today.

Notes

Chapter 1—In the Shadows of Progress
[1]Johan Huizinga, *In the Shadow of Tomorrow*, trans. J. H. Huizinga (New York: W. W. Norton and Company, 1964).
[2]Karl Löwith, *Nature, History and Existentialism* (Evanston, Illinois: Northwestern University Press, 1966), pp. 159-60.

Chapter 2—Ideology and Idolatry
[1]Quoted in Everett Crosby and Charles R. Webb, Jr., *Past as Prologue*, 2 vols. (New York: Irvington Publishers, 1973), 2:517.
[2]Psalm 115:5-8.

Chapter 3—The Ideology of Revolution
[1]Nicolai Gogol, *Dead Souls*, trans. George Reavey with an introduction by George Gibian (New York: W. W. Norton and Company, 1971).
[2]Groen van Prinsterer, *Grondsetsherziening en Eengezindheid* [*Constitutional Revision and Unanimity of Mind*] (Amsterdam: Johannus Müller, 1848), p. 479.
[3]Kolakowski has written *Main Currents of Marxism*, trans. P. S. Falla

(Oxford: Clarendon Press, 1978); *Toward a Marxist Humanism*, trans. Jane Zielonko Peel (New York: Grove Press, Inc., 1968); and *Der Mensch ohn Alternative: Von der Möglichkeit und Unmöglichkeit, Marxist zu sein* [*Man without an Alternative: On the Possibility and Impossibility of Being a Marxist*] (München: R. Piper & Co. Verlag, 1961).
Djilas's many books include *The Stone and the Violets*, trans. Lovett F. Edwards (New York: Harcourt Brace Jovanovich, 1972); *Conversations with Stalin*, trans. Michael B. Petrovich (New York: Harcourt, Brace & World, 1962); *Land without Justice*, intro. and notes William Jovanich (New York: Harcourt, Brace & Co., 1958); and *The New Class: An Analysis of the Communist System* (New York: Praeger, 1957).
Rudolf Bahro's works are *Elemente einer neuen Politik: Zum Verhältnis Von Ökologie und Socialismus* [*Elements of a New Politics: Towards a Relation between Ecology and Socialism*] (Berlin: Verlag Olle und Wolter, 1980); *Plädoyer fur schopferisch Initiative: Zur Kritik von Arbeitsbedingungen im Real existierenden Socialismus* [*Plea for Creative Initiative: Towards a Critique of Labor Conditions in Actually Existing Socialism*] (Köln: Bund-Verlag, 1980); and *The Alternative in Eastern Europe*, trans. David Fernbach (Oxford: NLB, 1978).
[4]V. I. Lenin, "The Tasks of the Youth Leagues," *Selected Works*, 3 vols. (Moscow: Foreign Languages Publishing House, 1961), 3:512.
[5]Quoted in David Shub, *Lenin: A Biography* (Garden City, New York: Doubleday & Company, Inc., 1951), p. 355. The selection is from Lenin's speech of 1920, "Left Wing Communism: An Infantile Disorder," which is reprinted in V. I. Lenin, *Selected Works*, vol. 3.
[6]Fyodor Dostoyevsky, *Crime and Punishment*, trans. with an intro. by David Magarshack (Baltimore, Maryland: Penguin Books, 1964), p. 277.
[7]Nikita Khrushchev, "On Peaceful Coexistence," *Foreign Affairs* 38 (October 1959). See also *Fundamentals of Marxism-Leninism* (Moscow: Foreign Languages Publishing House, 1961), pp. 565-84; and Nikita Khrushchev, *Conquest without War*, ed. N. H. Mager and Jacques Katel (New York: Simon and Schuster, 1961).
[8]Nikita Khrushchev in "On Peaceful Coexistence," p. 5.
[9]Quoted by Nikita Khrushchev in "On the Communist Program," Khrushchev's report on the Communist Party Program to the 22nd Congress of the Party (Moscow: Foreign Languages Publishing House, 1961), p. 27.
[10]Rudolf Bahro, *The Alternative in Eastern Europe*, p. 176.
[11]Ibid., p. 20.

[12]Ibid.

Chapter 4—The Ideology of Nation

[1]James Michener, *The Covenant* (New York: Random House, 1980).
[2]See chapter 3, "Calvinism and Politics," in Abraham Kuyper, *Lectures on Calvinism* (Grand Rapids, Mich.: Eerdmans, 1981).
[3]Matthew 16:25.
[4]Many advocate a boycott of South African energy. I believe, however, that a boycott could be counterproductive. Further foreign pressure on an economic level will possibly reinforce the feeling that as a nation South Africa "stands alone." A boycott would help to close the ranks— the *laager*—of the Afrikaners even more. That is my fear, at any rate.
[5]In *International Politics and the Demand for Global Justice* (Sioux Center, Iowa: Dordt College Press, 1981), p. 36, James Skillen states: "We see, then, that the goal of 'America first' or 'keeping the United States number one' cannot function as a meaningful goal of foreign policy." A highly recommended, anti-ideological book.
[6]Some examples of this can be found in Bertram Gross, *Friendly Fascism: The New Face of Power in America* (New York: M. Evans and Company, Inc., 1980).
[7]See James Tillman and Mary N. Tillman, *Why America Needs Racism and Poverty* (New York: Four Winds, 1973).

Chapter 5—The Ideology of Material Prosperity

[1]John Maynard Keynes, "The Economic Possibilities for Our Grand-children" (1930), *Essays in Persuasion* (New York: Harcourt, Brace & Co., 1932).
[2]Through devastation and the leveling of forests, the world's arable ground decreases 3 per cent every ten years. This figure is derived from the OECD report *Facing the Future* (Paris: OECD, 1979).
[3]United Nations, Report of the Secretary-General, *The Relationship between Disarmament and Development* (Study Series 5), 1982, p. 51.
[4]*The Global 2000 Report to the President* (Jimmy Carter) predicts that by the year 2000, 20 per cent of all plant and animal species and 40 per cent of the world's forests will be extinguished. (The Council on Environmental Quality and the Department of State, *The Global 2000 Report to the President: Entering the Twenty-First Century*, 3 vols. [New York: Penguin Books, 1982], 1:37, 23.)
[5]This was especially true in some European welfare states, such as Sweden, The Netherlands and Great Britain.

[6]Article 2 of the constitution of the European Economic Community states the following: "The Community shall have as its task . . . to promote throughout the Community a harmonious development of economic activities, a continuous and balanced expansion . . . and an accelerated raising of the standard of living." (Amos J. Paeslee, ed., *International Governmental Organizations: Constitutional Documents,* 5 vols. [The Hague: Martinus Nijhoff, 1974], 1:458.)

[7]Article 1 of the constitution of the Organization for Economic Cooperation and Development reads as follows: "Art. 1. The Aims of the Organization for Economic Co-operation and Development . . . shall be to promote policies designed: (a) to achieve the highest sustainable economic growth and a rising standard of living in Member countries." (Amos J. Paeslee, *International Governmental Organizations: Constitutional Documents,* 2:1155.)

Chapter 6—The Ideology of Guaranteed Security

[1]The figures come from SIPRI (Stockholm International Peace Research Institute).

[2]Niccolo Machiavelli, "The Art of War," *Machiavelli: The Chief Works and Others,* trans. Allan Gilbert (Durham, North Carolina: Duke University Press, 1965).

[3]Quoted by Robert Nisbet, *The Social Philosophers* (New York: Thomas Y. Crowell Company, 1973), p. 60.

[4]F. A. Aulard, ed., *Recueil des Actes du Comite de Salut Public [Record of the Acts of the Committee of Public Safety],* 28 vols. (Paris: Imprimerie Nationale, 1899), 6:72. The French text reads as follows:

La Convention nationale, après avoir entendu le rapport de son Comité de salute public, décrète:

Article 1er. Dès ce moment, jusqu'à celui où les ennemis auront été chassés du territoire de la République, tous les Francais sont en réquisition pout le service des armées.

Les jeunes gen iront au combat; les hommes mariés forgeront les armes et transporteront les subsistances; les femmes feront des tentes, des habits et serviront dans les hôpitaux; les enfants mettront les vieux linges en charpie; les viellards se feront porter sur les places publiques pour exciter le courage des guerriers, prêcher la haine des rois et l'unité de la République.

[5]Carl von Clausewitz, *On War,* edited by Anatol Rapoport (Baltimore, Maryland: Penguin Books, 1968).

[6]Nobel also built a number of luxurious resorts on the Mediterranean

Sea, where in the midst of the overwhelming beauty of nature people could commit suicide in peace.

[7]Among other books van Vollenhoven has written *The Law of Peace*, trans. W. Carter (London: MacMillan, 1936); and *Scope and Content of International Law* (Leiden: E. J. Brill, 1932).

[8]United Nations, *The Relationship between Disarmament and Development*, Chart II.2, p. 18.

[9]Henry Kissinger, *The White House Years* (Boston: Little, Brown and Company, 1979).

[10]Henry Kissinger, *The White House Years*, p. 217.

[11]According to the Olof Palme report *Common Security*, the estimated value of net weapons exports of the developed countries to the rest of the world rose (in 1978 prices) from 6.3 billion dollars in 1970 to 16.1 billion dollars per year in 1977-79. (The Independent Commission on Disarmament and Security Issues, *Common Security: A Blueprint for Survival* [New York: Simon and Schuster, 1982], p. 94.)

[12]*Time*, 18 April 1983, p. 21.

[13]Quoted in Richard Barnet, *The Economy of Death* (New York: Atheneum, 1969), p. 9.

[14]A recent report of the Christian Democratic Appeal, currently the governing party in The Netherlands, is a case in point.

[15]Jeremiah 7:31 (see 2 Kings 23:10). Other references to Molech are found in Leviticus, 1 and 2 Kings, Jeremiah, Amos and Acts.

[16]Quoted in John Weldon and Clifford Wilson, *Approaching the Decade of Shock* (San Diego: Master Books, 1978).

[17]Even the pursuit of disarmament can be purely ideological. For example, an ideology is at work if the disarmament movement gives out false information, or if it installs its own image of the enemy, as when it portrays America as the sinister threat and the Soviet Union as a benevolent friend.

[18]*Torah* means "law." In our Western view of things, every use of the word *law* has the connotation of a restriction of freedom, an imposition of rules which takes away our liberty. But for Jewish people the Torah means first and foremost a path to walk on, a "direction," a route secure from harm. It is the path along which blessing comes. This is the meaning I have in mind here.

[19]The vast diversity of modern theologies—such as the theology of revolution, black theology, liberation theology and feminist theology—all betray self-chosen goals out of which the biblical message is read and "understood." They are a mirror of the ideological fragmentation of

the church.
[20]See Colossians 2:15.

Chapter 7—The Monstrous Alliance

[1]Revelation 6:1-8.
[2]United Nations, *The Relationship between Disarmament and Development*, p. 43.
[3]Alva Myrdal, *The Game of Disarmament* (New York: Pantheon Books, 1976), p. 24.
[4]Robert Triffin, "Gold and the Dollar Crisis: Yesterday and Tomorrow," *Essays in International Finance* 132 (December 1978), p. 4.
[5]Ibid.
[6]*Time,* 10 January 1983, p. 43.
[7]Barbara Ward, "Another Chance for the North?" *Foreign Affairs* 59 (Winter 1980/81).

Chapter 8—Hope Awakens Life

[1]G. K. Chesterton, *Orthodoxy* (Garden City, New York: Image Books, 1959).
[2]Ibid., pp. 28-29.
[3]Colossians 2:15 (The New English Bible [Oxford: Oxford University Press, 1970]).
[4]*Mammon* is the biblical name for the idol of money, *Molech* for the idol of military power, and *Baal* for the idol of natural survival and fertility.
[5]Friedrich Weinreb, *Ik Die Verborgen Ben* (The Hague: Servire, 1974).
[6]Esther 4:14.
[7]Weinreb, *Ik Die Verborgen Ben,* p. 89.
[8]See Amos 1 and 2.
[9]Deuteronomy 20:14.
[10]See Isaiah 8 and 9.
[11]Psalm 68:17. See also Psalms 46, 82 and 89.
[12]United Nations, *The Relationship between Disarmament and Development*, p. 64.
[13]Isaiah 2:4. Many detailed conversion plans have been developed (see, for example, George McRobie, *Small Is Possible* [San Francisco: Harper and Row, 1981]). The United Nations report *The Relationship between Disarmament and Development* (p. 90ff.) contains a calculation by the American economist Wassily Leontief which traces both an accelerated arming of the world and a "disarmament scenario" in which military expenditures drop to 75 per cent and ultimately to 60 per cent of their

current relative volume. In the first case, by the year 2000 national incomes per capita of the population would drop 33 per cent; in the second case it would rise more than 160 per cent. The corresponding figures for the poor Asian countries are 2 per cent and 47 per cent.
[14]Genesis 2:15.